FORTY YEARS' PROBATION

THE LIFE OF TONY HUEREÑA
A TRUE STORY OF GOD'S CALLING

FORTY YEARS' PROBATION

THE LIFE OF TONY HUEREÑA
A TRUE STORY OF GOD'S CALLING

TONY J. HUEREÑA

EQUIP PRESS
Colorado Springs

FORTY YEARS' PROBATION

Forty Years' Probation: The Life of Tony Huereña- A True Story of God's Calling
Copyright © 2020 Tony J. Huereña

All rights reserved. No part of this publication may be reproduced, distributed, ortransmitted in any form or by any means, without prior written permission.

Scripture quotations marked (ESV) are taken from The ESV® Bible (The Holy Bible, English Standard Version®) copyright © 2001 by Crossway, a publishing minis-try of Good News Publishers. ESV® Text Edition: 2011. The ESV® text has beenreproduced in cooperation with and by permission of Good News Publishers.
Unauthorized reproduction of this publication is prohibited. Used by permission.
All rights reserved.

Scripture quotations marked (KJV) are taken from the King James Bible. Accessedon Bible Gateway at www.BibleGateway.com.

Scripture quotations marked (NASB) are taken from the New American Standard Bible® (NASB), copyright © 1960, 1962, 1963, 1968, 1971, 1972, 1973, 1975,
1977, 1995 by The Lockman Foundation, www.Lockman.org. Used by permission.

Scripture quotations marked (NIV) are taken from the Holy Bible, New International Version. Copyright © 1973, 1978, 1984, 2011 by Biblica, Inc.® Used by permission.
All rights reserved worldwide.

Scripture quotations marked (NKJV) are taken from the New King James Version®. Copyright © 1982 by Thomas Nelson, Inc. Used by permission. All rights reserved.

Scripture quotations marked (NLT) are taken from the Holy Bible, New Living Translation, copyright © 1996, 2004, 2015 by Tyndale House Foundation. Usedby permission of Tyndale House Publishers, Inc., Carol Stream, Illinois 60188.
Allrights reserved.

Scripture quotations marked (NRSV) are taken from the New Revised Standard Version Bible, copyright © 1989 the Division of Christian Education of the National

Scripture quotations taken from the Amplified® Bible (AMP), Copyright © 2015 by The Lockman Foundation Used by permission. www.Lockman.org

First Edition: 2020
Forty Years' Probation / Tony J. Huereña
Paperback ISBN: 978-1-951304-29-4
eBook ISBN: TBD

ENDORSEMENT

"I have known Tony for quite a long time on many levels and have seen him evolve. This book is about hope, forgiveness, and the power of God's goodness. I highly recommend this book for people looking for hope and second chance in life."

Francis F Joseph MD JD
Medical Director
Certified Health and Hospital Law

DEDICATION

First of all, I would like to thank my Lord and Savior, Jesus, for salvation, deliverance, and patience with me.

To my beautiful mother, Virginia, and my sisters, Mary, Elizabeth, and Eva.

To the many people that God has used along the way to mold me into the man I am today:

Pastor Steve, Pastor Sonny, Nicky, Pastor Al, Pastor Paul, Pastor Mark, Pastor Jefferson, and Pastor Randy.

To my son, Robert, my daughter, Linda, and son, Teddy.

Special thanks to the many people who have come alongside us during this journey in life:

Francesco, Brock and Amy, Sam, Surrinder, Nod, Jag, Jas, Perry, and many more.

And to the most important person on this earth, my beautiful and lovely wife. Carolina, I love you and thank you for the support, love, sacrifice, and willingness to do what God wants. I appreciate you!

CONTENTS

ENDORSEMENT 5

DEDICATION 7

PRELUDE 11

CHAPTER I: Going Back in Time (1957-1974) 13

CHAPTER II: A Second Chance (1974-1979) 19

CHAPTER III: On the Run (1980-1984) 27

CHAPTER IV: The Assignment of Seeing the Heart 43

CHAPTER V: The Heart of Gang Members (1991-1999) 53

CHAPTER VI: The Heart of the Corporate World (1999-2002) 65

CHAPTER VII: The Heart of the Entertainers (2002-2007) 73

Chapter VIII: Heart of the Clean and Sober (2007-2011) 82

Chapter IX: Heart of the Homeless (2012-2015) 88

Chapter X: Come Full Circle (2015-2018) 96

Conclusion 105

PRELUDE

The number forty is used many times in the Bible and generally symbolizes a period of testing, trial, or probation. God often still tests His people. At times, this testing is seen as punishment, reproof, or correction. But sometimes this testing is to see if the person will seek God and still praise Him even in the storms of life. The number forty also represents transition or change—the concept of renewal, a new beginning.

In 1976, at age nineteen, God spoke to me and said, "I have called you to preach to a backslidden, stiff-necked, rebellious people, and to preach the message of the end times."

One night in December 2016, I couldn't sleep, so I got up to pray.

God asked me, "Do you remember when I called you?"

I said, "Yes."

He said, "What year was that and what did I say to you?"

"It was 1976.

"Yes, it was 1976. What is this year?"

I said, "2016."

"How many years is it from 1976 to present?

I said, "forty years."

He said, "It has been forty years. I am about to do a new thing in your life. I have called you and your wife for such a time as this. It is time to fulfill the assignment I have given you."

CHAPTER 1

GOING BACK IN TIME (1957-1974)

It was a hot summer evening in Las Vegas, NV, 1974. I was sixteen years old. The police had just pulled me over. Six police officers beat me down, smashing my head into the hood of my '69 Caprice. They forced handcuffs onto my wrists and shoved me into the back seat of the police car. I'd been here before. I remember hearing the words, "I knew I'd catch a dumb Mexican today."

My mother, Virginia, was born in La Veta, Colorado to Porfilio and Margarita Pacheco and was adopted by her father's sister, Sophia. She was raised in the small town of Walsenburg, Colorado. My father, Emiterio Huereña, was born to Epifano and Adella Huereña and raised in Trinidad, Colorado. My mother married my father at a young age and moved to St. Louis, Missouri. My sisters, Carol and Elizabeth, and I were born in St.

Louis. My sister, Eva, was born later. When I was three years old, my mother and father got divorced.

My father was a womanizer and would abuse my mother, so we went to Walsenburg to stay with my grandmother on a farm. My mother and father divorced, and it would be a few years before we would see our father again. My mother had a relative, Lillian, who was adopted by my mother's grandmother's mother. My mother went to Denver to stay with Aunt Lillian until she could find employment and later married Joe.

I hung out with Priscilla, Barbara, Butch, Lola, and Sally. Priscilla and I were the same age and were always together. This was during the time when John F. Kennedy and Martin Luther King Jr. were assassinated. I still remember the riots.

Our stepfather, Joe, was an alcoholic and very abusive, and he disliked my elder sister, Carol. He would hit us and come home drunk and beat my mother. I remember my mother being pregnant, laying on the ground in puddles of blood in convulsions. We learned to fear Joe. This would be the beginning of many years of resentment, anger, and rage that would lead me down the wrong road.

Eventually, my mother left Joe and we moved to Pueblo, Colorado. At age eleven, I began drinking alcohol and saw some of the older guys shooting heroin and doing cocaine. We formed a gang and began stealing, having keg parties, and going to parties. Fighting became a big part of my life, and I expressed a lot of anger and bitterness.

The Raza Movement was going on. Carol began dating her soon-to-be husband, Andrew Casados. They were older than me and were all in the Brown Berets (Viva la Raza). I admired the older guys. I felt like this was what I was born for—partying, girlfriends, and fighting. I hated authority and was always being called into the principal's office. He would say, "Which paddle do you want today?" "Surprise me!" I'd reply. I didn't care anymore and felt hatred building inside of me.

At age fourteen, my father came to see us and asked my mother to give him a chance, so we moved back to Denver. I was so happy because I wanted to be near my dad. But all I knew was partying with the older guys. We burglarized stores. I was always the shortest guy, so I would go up to a group of guys and hit the biggest one, and we would start a riot.

I hated other nationalities and any authority. Partying and girls were my favorite things in life. We put gasoline in bottles with a rag at the top, and then we'd light it and throw it at police cars just for the fun of it. An old high school love of my mother (Fred) called and asked her to marry him and move to Las Vegas, Nevada. She accepted and we packed up and moved to Las Vegas.

I could see it now (I thought)—limousines, glitter, my name in neon lights, glamour, and fame. I was about to find out what real life was about. For a few weeks, we moved into a house in the heart of the west side, a neighborhood populated by African Americans. On the first day, I went to school and looked around the classroom—not one Latino. Remember, I had known nothing but the gang, the brown Pride and Prejudice. I walked out of school and never went back.

My stepdad, Fred, got me a job at a casino in Las Vegas. I worked for Michael Gaughn. My stepdad had a son named Freddy who came out to Vegas to live with us. My stepdad felt he would rather have us stay at home and drink and smoke weed rather than doing it outside the house.

My sister, Carol, and her husband, Andrew, and their two children moved to Las Vegas. My stepdad, my stepbrother, Freddy, my stepdad's brother and nephew, and I worked at the Royal Inn Casino. I soon found real life existed, and that life was to include all nationalities. I had a new group of friends. After work, we all got high, drank whiskey and beer, and snorted cocaine. I found a Latina girlfriend and other girlfriends of different nationalities. My first young love during my time in Vegas was Debbie at the age of 16.

I got my first car, a '69 Chevy Caprice, and Freddy purchased a Nova. We worked every day, and partied. Our uncle, Ernie, had an old '38 Pontiac with suicide doors. We carried guns, shotguns, and baseball bats and drove under the influence of drugs and alcohol. At sixteen years old, I would go into 7-11 and purchase liquor. We cruised Las Vegas Boulevard and Fremont Street, meeting girls and partying at Lake Mead.

The police were very prejudiced. Whenever I was pulled over in my low rider, the first thing the police officer said was, "I knew I'd get me a Mexican today." I'd fight with that officer and end up getting beat by several policemen. I never knew how to surrender and shut up. I was so full of bitterness, anger, and hatred, and didn't care about life. I totaled my '69 Caprice and then bought a brand new '75 Ford Courier pickup, custom painted. I only had that for a short period before I wrecked it.

I once drove at high speed, and a young couple was walking down the street. The man hollered out to me to slow down. I stopped, made a U-turn, pulled up beside them, and asked what he said. He said to slow down, and I called him a punk. He went to grab me. I pulled a gun out, made him get on his stomach, and began shooting all around him.

I drove home, pulled up into the driveway, and threw the gun into the empty field next to our house. The police showed up and searched my car, but they didn't find it. The juvenile judge was Judge Mendoza. He was known as the "Hanging Judge" and had sent his own daughter up for drugs.

At least once a month, I was taken to Juvenile Detention. It was like a high to me to fight with police officers and break the law, to push the envelope. My stepdad would say, "You're like a cat with nine lives. You always come out smelling like a rose." The juvenile system tried everything to help me. I was out of control, constantly wrecking cars, getting caught with guns in my car, and keeping a trunk full of drugs. Somehow there was always a loophole.

I stole Freddie's car one night and drove past McCarran International Airport, watching airplanes take off. I thought, *These people are free. I'm stuck and can't escape this life.* I was watching a plane near the fence; as it came down the runway, I thought, *If*

I plan this right, I could drive through the wire-linked fence, drive into the path of the airplane, the airplane will hit the car, the car will explode, and I'll die. I drove through the wire-link fence, my head hit the steering wheel, and I got knocked out. I ended up in a padded cell. My probation officer really liked me and tried everything to help me with my issues.

The courts were waiting for my eighteenth birthday to send me to the Nevada State Penitentiary. I was staying with my sister then. [Thank you, Carol, for always being there for me.] After staying out all night, I went home to take a shower to get ready to leave again. Carol was very sick and said somebody was coming from a nearby church to pray for her. I finished getting ready and came out to the living room to find some ladies laying hands on my sister and speaking in tongues. I didn't know what was going on. Carol was healed instantly.

One of those ladies was Sister Moore, a 91-year-old woman who had been an evangelist her whole life. Carol introduced me to them. Sister Moore pointed her bony little finger at me and said, "You, young man, you have a calling in your life, a calling to be an evangelist. Do you know Nicky Cruz?" I said no (I didn't know Nicky at the time), and she said, "You have a calling to be like Nicky Cruz. The Lord showed me you are having problems with the law. God will take care of that, and the girl you are dating, you need to cut her loose."

CHAPTER II

A SECOND CHANCE (1974-1979)

I had been fasting for a few days, and the Lord spoke to me and said, "I have called you to preach the last-day message. I have called you to preach to a stiff-necked, rebellious, backslidden generation."

We were invited to go to church, so my sister, my brother-in-law, and I went that weekend. After the sermon, Pastor Nadeau had an altar call. I went up, sobbing, and knelt down. People surrounded me, laying hands on me and praying. I was slain under the power of the Holy Spirit. I woke up soaking wet from the top of my head to the soles of my shoes, speaking in tongues. I felt like the weight of everything was taken off my shoulders. God changed me instantly.

I cut Debbie loose, stopped using and selling drugs and drinking, and began attending church. I felt different. I literally "felt

God" in my life. Sister Moore took me under her wing, laying hands on me, and imparted the gift of evangelism into my life. We were together for hours and hours at a time. She taught me and shared her experiences with me. She'd been an evangelist all her life and preached in tent revivals with people like Catherine Coleman, Billy Graham, and others.

We fellowshipped with a few positive, saved, and sanctified brothers and sisters. Freddie and I made a makeshift pulpit in our bedroom and pretended to be preachers. I cut my hair and God changed my life. My probation officer, who had tried everything to help me, saw a big change in my life. My family was so happy, and my mother was beyond happy. She has always loved me unconditionally and was always praying for me.

Carol and Andrew were planning to move to Colorado. I wanted to go to Colorado with them, but the last time I had seen Judge Mendoza, he said if he ever saw me in his courtroom, he would lock me up and throw away the key. I spoke to my probation officer, Linda, and told her I'd like to move to Colorado with my sister.

As I stood before Judge Mendoza, he said, "You know, Tony, you have been here in Las Vegas less than two years and you have a record longer than the Las Vegas strip. My probation officer requested the courts dismiss my sentence and allow me to go to Colorado. "The state wouldn't have to deal with him anymore," she said, and told the judge of the change she had witnessed.

The judge stood quietly for what seemed like an eternity. Then he asked if I had anything to say. I got up and gave my testimony.

He dismissed my cases and told me to leave the state of Nevada. Little did I know that Sister Moore's prophecy was about to come to pass.

We moved to Colorado. Andrew's mother was attending a small church in Pueblo, so we began attending Pastor McCoy's church. Elizabeth and her husband, Gilbert, Carol and Andrew, and I were very happy. Pastor McCoy was an outgoing, happy, excited pastor who preached under the power of the Holy Ghost. He was the pastor in the phone book, but Sister McCoy was the "real pastor." She was a very controlling person.

I was about four months old in the Lord when Pastor McCoy asked me to come up one Sunday morning to give my testimony and lead song service. He said, "Tony came to us from Las Vegas. Can anything good come from Las Vegas? We have Tony!" Soon Pastor McCoy asked me to start helping to lead song service regularly.

I got a job at a steak house. The only experience I had was in Las Vegas at the casinos. The Lord moved me to begin preaching in the county jail, and I saw guys there I was in the gang with a few years earlier.

There were some good people in the church. A girl named Jeri attended. She liked me, and I liked her too. I started a youth group called "Young People's Outreach for Christ." The goal was to disciple young people and get them plugged into a church.

Benito and Orlinda and their daughter, Eliza, attended the church. They knew I needed a house to have the "youth wrap sessions." They offered their home for the groups once a week. Benito started helping me with the jail services. The youth group was growing, and we were reaching many people. Quite a few of them were my homeboys and homegirls I hung out with in the past.

The problem we experienced was that most of the pastors in the small town of Pueblo came from the same church. Division came in and people started moving to other parts of town, opening churches, and taking a few people with them. Pretty soon, you had a few churches with a few people, and they told their members, "Don't go to so-and-so church. You'll have the judgment of God against you." We tried taking the youth from the group to church, and people judged them for the way they dressed, their hair, their lifestyles, etc.

I "felt" like it was God's plan for Eliza and me to get married. We got married and worked together in Young People's Outreach for Christ. One night, Pastor asked me to come up to the pulpit and give my testimony and lead song service. Afterward, Pastor Rose, an elderly lady, asked if I would come to her church in Trinidad, Colorado (at the border of New Mexico and Colorado) to give my testimony and to preach. I accepted.

That night in Trinidad, I was in the church parsonage waiting to be introduced (do churches even have parsonages anymore?). I was so nervous I walked back and forth praying and sweating. I had memorized the whole chapter of St. John 14 and never even preached on it. Only a handful of people were there that night, which was fine with me. I was very nervous. After the service, Pastor

Rose asked me to come back and preach a revival. I asked, "What's a revival?" She told me it would be for a week and I would preach every night. I wasn't sure about this. She said, "Tony, you're called to be an evangelist. You're anointed by God." I still wasn't sure, but I'd heard that before, so I accepted.

While waiting for revival to begin, I felt the Lord dealing with me about my job cooking at the steak house. I told the owner I was quitting to be in ministry full time. He said, "Tony, we love you. Why don't you just work part time?" I declined and set out on a mission.

I fasted and prayed for a few days, and one night the Lord said to me, "I have called you to preach to a stiff-necked, rebellious, backsliding generation." All I could do was lie there and weep. During this time, our daughter, Linda Stella Huereña, was born.

One night, Eliza and I went to the park, which had a bridge going over a pond. At the end of the small bridge was a nice stage under a rainbow-shaped covering. We were standing at the edge of the pond. As though it was daylight, I could see people walking in groups over the bridge to the stage with their hands up, as if they were surrendering. I stood up all night pondering this vision.

The next day I called Parks and Recreation and asked what it would take to have a church service at the park. The guy in charge was a guy I went to school with, imagine that! [Thank you, Lord.] He said, "Tony, I'll give you a permit for any park in town all summer, as long as it fits our schedule." So I scheduled most parks. I wanted to reach souls on all sides of town.

We arrived at the church the day the revival was scheduled to start. We would spend the week in the parsonage. Benito and Orlinda, my in-laws, went with us. That night, I was expecting just a few people. I was in the parsonage praying, nervous and pacing. I was introduced and came out to the platform. To my surprise, the church was packed. Eliza sang a song; she had a beautiful voice.

A young man named Nick Sortino from New York sang a few songs. I got up to preach. The anointing of the Holy Spirit hit, and we had a Holy Ghost-lead service. Every night, Eliza sang, Nick sang, and I preached. That week, I saw thirteen cavities filled right before my eyes. A person got out of a wheelchair and walked. A man with one leg shorter than the other had a special shoe and came up for prayers. We sat him in a chair, prayed, and watched his leg grow to the size of the other.

At the beginning of the revival, a young lady named Julie came up for prayer. She said her husband, Joe, was an alcoholic and was controlling and jealous. She wanted us to pray for him. Another young lady came up for prayer for her husband, Greg. As I was praying for her, I saw in a vision a house with a picket fence around the yard, a big picture window with chairs in a circle in the middle of the room, and a chair in the middle of the circle. I told her what I saw, and she said, "Yes, my husband is into witchcraft and they have meetings at our house. They set up the chairs like that."

I anointed a piece of cloth with olive oil, prayed over it, and told her to put it under her husband's pillowcase. Within ninety days, he would be saved and he'd be a deacon in a church. One day, she called me all excited and said, "Brother Tony, I just found your phone number. Guess what?"

I said, "What?"

"Greg got saved and is a deacon of the church."

God is faithful!

Another young lady brought her mother up for prayer. I looked into this mother's eyes and the Lord said to me, "Don't anoint her with oil; don't put your hands on her." I stretched out my hands, without touching her, and prayed (I didn't know what was going on). She fell flat on her back and was shaking. She moved along the aisle like a snake, cursing. I told a few ushers to hold her, and I stretched out my hands and spoke to the demons. She was set free.

On the last night of the revival, Julie was praying for her husband again when Joe came in the door drunk. I had already preached, and we were singing a few songs. The Holy Spirit was moving; we were having a time in the Lord. Joe hollered out, "You, preacher, I want to talk to you!"

I told them to continue allowing the Holy Spirit to move. I went to the side of the altar with Joe and he said, "I've been watching you all week and I want what you have." I called Julie up, laid hands on Joe, and prayed. He fell down and woke up sober. The Holy Spirit revealed to me they would be pastors. The last time I saw them, they were still pastoring a church.

I started traveling all around Colorado preaching revivals. I saw souls being saved, demon-possessed people set free, and many, many miracles. A few months after that first revival, the singer, Nick

Sortino, called and said he had moved to Denver and was attending a big church. He directed a choir with about twenty young, Holy Ghost-filled people, and he asked me to come preach. What a Holy Ghost service we had! Nick said whenever we preached, he could bring the choir and the church bus and come to minister and evangelize with us. Baby Linda enjoyed being on a bus around a bunch of young people singing. She would be so happy around all of this. We began taking the choir on our revivals. God is awesome.

Eliza and I were fighting a lot. She felt like I wanted to be with every woman who came up for prayer. Insecurity got the best of her. I started slowing down on the preaching, went back to work, and became the kitchen manager of a restaurant. The fighting got worse between Eliza and me. One night she took Linda and left. I knew it was over.

CHAPTER III
ON THE RUN (1980-1984)

I answered the phone, and it was the District Attorney of San Bernardino County. "Mr. Huerena, one of the victims of your case has died. We don't know what we're charging you with, but you need to leave Las Vegas and turn yourself in to our office in San Bernardino or we'll put out a nationwide fugitive warrant for you." I said, "If you want me, come and get me."

I stayed the night at Elizabeth's house until I could get a hotel room the next day. When I arrived, Jeri was out sitting on the front porch babysitting my nephews. As we talked, Eliza drove up, and I said to myself, *You want to accuse me; I'll give you a reason to.* I put my arm around Jeri. Eliza and I had a few words, and she left. I started drinking that night.

A few days later, I drove past Eliza's parents' house a few times, entertaining the thought of just going in and taking my daughter.

Instead, I decided to just leave town and stay away. Jeri was going through some tough times; she was pregnant and had no plans. I rented a hotel room and asked her to stay with me. When I got to Vegas, I got a job and an apartment and sent for Jeri. But I was backsliding and was back into drinking. All I did was drink and work.

Many people asked how I could be in the ministry full time, see miracles, and then backslide and move away from God. Remember, I was just a few months in the Lord when I began in the ministry. I had no foundation. All I knew before was the street life. I had no maturity to fall back on. When my daughter was taken out of my life, I didn't know how to deal with it. I soon lost my job. For a while, I went from job to job, and then I got an apartment with Elizabeth.

Jeri and her daughter, Jessica, soon went back to Colorado. A few days after she got back to Pueblo, my cousin called me and said, "I saw Jeri with her daughter's dad last night." Ten months later, Jeri called me and said, "I had your son. I named him after you, Anthony James Huereña Jr." I told her he wasn't my son; he was Phillip's son. Jeri really did love me, but I was no good for her or anybody. I was about to go down a road that I thought I would never come out of. I was busted, disgusted, and couldn't be trusted.

The Bible says in St. Matthew 12:43-45, "When an impure spirit comes out of a person, it goes into the desert, seeking rest but finds none. Then it says, 'I will return to the person I came from.' So it returns and finds its former home empty, swept, and in order. The spirit finds seven other spirits more evil than itself, and they all enter the person and live there. And so that person is worse off than before."

By the grace of God, I made it back. The apartment we were living in was a world of its own, right behind the world of glitter and glamor (The Strip). Sections of apartments surrounded Circle Park, and each section was divided by nationalities: African Americans, Puerto Ricans, Mexicans, Asians, etc. At the time, this area was called Heroin Heights. I had a Mexican gang after me and an African American gang out to get me.

Many times, I knew only the angels of God and the grace of God had gotten me out of situations. One time I went to the liquor store and the apartment manager's son lived right next to the stairs that lead to my apartment. The stairs came to the second floor, and there were five doors before my door. My apartment was at the end of the corridor. I was heading toward the stairs and saw a few of the guys who were after me, some African Americans and Mexicans. They called me and started coming toward me. I told them I would go one-on-one with every one of them, but I wouldn't fight all of them.

I was backing up the stairs away from them, and they were following me. I had my brim on, and as I got to the top of the stairs, I felt a knife cut the top of my brim off. I ducked and was pulled backward at the top of the stairs by someone. I saw a guy with a big knife in one hand and a hammer in the other, and he was swinging both at me. I was doing the best I could. The others got to me, and the next thing I knew, the manager's son and a bunch of his friends came out of his apartment and helped me take these guys on.

Many people were out to get me, so I practiced escaping from my apartment. I would run down the hallway to the bedroom, jump out the window onto the canvas below, and jump down to the ground and run down the alley. I kept my apartment dark and spent days in the dark, drinking and sitting there with a gun. A few times I had the gun to my head and couldn't pull the trigger.

One day, I went with my Uncle Ernie to a friend's house a block over from the apartment. We went inside and had a few beers. This guy had many things that could be sold. When he went to work, I went back to his house later that evening and carried quite a few items back to my apartment. I made about seven trips and even took the beer from his refrigerator.

A few people partied with me at the apartment. I went to the restroom, came out, and the cops were in the house with the guy I stole all this stuff from. They asked if he could identify any of his belongings. He started pointing out the items, and I said, "And don't forget the beer in the refrigerator." For some reason, the guy didn't press charges.

I soon ran into Ron, an old friend I used to party with when I was a teenager. He and his sister, Sharon, were moving into a house together. He asked if I could help them move. We drank and partied and moved all their stuff into their house. Ron was the brother of Dennis, Carol's ex-husband. I knew all of the family except for Sharon. Somehow, I ended up with Sharon, and she got pregnant and had our son Robert. I was into snorting coke, drinking, and whatever else life brought.

Sharon was a great woman, a hard worker, and very patient with me. I couldn't be a husband or father and was not a very good human, period. Sharon worked every day, and all I thought about was what "I" wanted. I drank whiskey all day, worked, and partied. I met a guy at the restaurant where I worked whose brother was a professional gambler. He taught me a few things about gambling in the small casinos.

I also met Earl, who had a house full of hookers he was pimping out. Earl and I would burglarize houses, pull some armed robberies, and party. One day, Sharon was working. Elizabeth and Sharon's birthday were on the same day, so Elizabeth's boyfriend and I decided to have a party for the two of them. We were in Sharon's 63 Chevy and went and got a few cases of beer and some bottles of Jack Daniels; I was snorting some coke.

We stopped at a gas station and the subject of LA came up, so we started driving there and got into an accident. The highway patrol later told me that along the way, I was so high I'd jack-knifed a car. When I came to, we had a blowout. I got out of the car; the right fender was rubbing against the tire. I pried it, put the spare tire on, and saw a gas station and bar up ahead. We went into the bar and started drinking a little while. I got up, went to the restroom, came out, and my sister's boyfriend was nowhere in the bar. I went outside and found him with two guys on him. I drove up to him, got him in the car, and we took off—going in the wrong direction (toward Vegas).

By now, it was dark outside. Next thing I knew, a helicopter above shined a spotlight on us, and highway patrol cars, sheriff cars, and state patrols were behind us. I drove for a while with the spotlight on us. Many thoughts went through my mind: *What shall I do, keep going until I run out of gas or stop and just let them shoot and kill me?*

I drove for what seemed like hours, stretching my arm out the window, flipping them off, music playing, and with no idea what to do. I finally pulled over, in the middle of nowhere. There we were, surrounded by all these sheriffs, state police, and the helicopter hovering over us with the spotlight on us.

I thought, *Just start running and it will all be over soon.*

"Driver, get out of the car slowly with your hands up." As I did, I saw every officer with guns aimed right at me. "Get down on your knees with your hands behind your head," I heard someone say.

I got down on my knees with my hands behind my head.

"Now, lie down flat on your stomach."

I did. I'd had handcuffs on many, many times, but this time, it felt different. The handcuffs felt so cold, and if I ever felt like a dog, it was now. I was yanked up to my feet so hard I felt my arm was broke. The guy in charge questioned me. "Why didn't you stop when you jack-knifed that vehicle, and why did you run over those two guys in the parking lot at the bar?"

I stood quietly. This was the only time I remember ever being quiet and surrendering peacefully.

I went to court, not knowing what to expect, and talked the judge into letting me go back to Las Vegas. I assured him I would come back for my scheduled court date. I know it was only the hand of God working one more time in my life. Soon after I went back to Las Vegas, I received a call from the DA in San Bernardino saying one person from the accident died and I was to turn myself in or I would have a fugitive warrant on me. I said, "Come and get me!"

I met an Italian guy (I'll just call him Bill) who had a lot of friends. We hit it off quickly. One day, Bill said, "Hey, I know where we can get thousands of dollars' worth of Sherm; it will be very easy."

I asked, "Where?"

"At a guy's house they call the Godfather."

I was in and said, "Let's go."

We went to the house and walked up to the front door. I broke the window next to the door and unlocked the door. He led me to the freezer, and we took a big plastic bag out and looked in it. I had never seen Sherm before (this was a drug used to tranquilize animals and for embalming); there was a lot of it in the bag. We slipped off into the darkness of Sin City, made some money, and partied with many people for a few days.

One morning at my apartment, I heard a knock on the door. It was Bill asking if he could use my shower. I said yes and told him I was going to walk down the alley to the liquor store.

I picked up some beer and Jack Daniels and then spotted a Mercedes Benz parked outside my apartment as I was coming back down the alley. I ducked behind a building and saw some guys dragging Bill out of my apartment and beating on him. I didn't think playing the hero was the best idea, so I went back to the liquor store, called Carol, and asked her to give me a ride to the airport. I left for Colorado. This time I had a hit out on me and a nationwide fugitive warrant issued for my arrest.

So there I was on the run, and I would spend the next few years moving back and forth from Vegas to Colorado. I was in Colorado around Halloween and hung out with Butch. I worked with him at a decorating company every year from Halloween to New Year's. We decorated malls, streets, and mansions up in the mountains.

We were on Larimer Street, where there's nothing but bars, drunks, and dancing. We worked all day, and at the end of the week, we had enough money to pay our bar tabs. Back then, Larimer was a notorious place. Every bar jukebox had the song by Kris Kristofferson (*Why Me, Lord*) about a backslider coming back to God. I would walk into bars wearing my brim, my dress pants, suspenders, Stacey Adams, and my spaghetti tie. I would walk up to the pool table and throw everybody's quarters off the pool table and slap my quarter down.

Many times, I found myself surrounded by a few guys with guns pointed at my head. I would start swinging on them, and sometimes they pistol-whipped me instead of shooting me, which was the grace of God.

One time, I went into the bar and sat where I could see everything behind me through the mirrors. A woman was sitting at a booth by herself. She smiled at me, so I had the bartender take her what she was drinking. I sent her another one, and the third one I took over to her. We talked for a while, and, suddenly, I felt an arm go around my neck and a hand on my belt, and I went flying over the booth and the bar. I could hear bullets flying all around me. I found out later the bartender saw the woman's husband walk in. He saw me sitting with his wife at the booth, so the bartender grabbed me and threw me over the bar to save my life, again, the grace of God. Many times, I would get into fights, get shot at, and get pistol-whipped. A few times, I went to Pueblo, Colorado and got my old job back cooking at the restaurant.

One night, I was working the graveyard shift and two police officers walked in. The manager met them at the door. I was watching through the pass-through counter, but I could tell they weren't there to eat. I ran to the back door and it was locked. I came back to the line, but by then, one officer was at one end of the line and the other was at the other end. They both had their guns pointed at me and told me to walk to the end of the kitchen. They handcuffed me and took me to jail.

I awaited extradition to the state of California. For some reason, they didn't come for me and I was released. I went back to Las Vegas and God sent a beautiful couple—Ted and Isie and their family. God is like that; when you have a calling on your life, He will not leave you alone. To this day, they are part of my life.

I stayed at my sister's house for a few months and worked at a casino. I had just left for work at 5:30 a.m., and the police were tipped off that I was in Vegas. They went to my sister's house looking through every room for me. They came to the casino and arrested me. Once again, I awaited extradition, and once again, on the thirtieth day, I was released.

I ran again to Colorado and got my old job back as kitchen manager. I hired a cousin as dishwasher and picked him up one morning for work. On the way, we approached a high school. He said, "Pull over, I see a friend of mine and need to talk to her." We pulled into the parking lot. After we left and drove a block, the police pulled us over. I asked why we were being pulled over, and he said, "For loitering on a school parking lot." One of the police officers said, "You know what? You're going to jail, and you're going to wash my car when you get there." I told him his mama was going to wash his car.

For some reason, I stood before the judge immediately. I told him I was the manager of the restaurant. Since it was just a ticket for loitering on a public school lot, I asked if I could pay the ticket at a later date, and he let me go. My cousin went with me to pay the ticket. In front of the courthouse was a long set of stairs leading to the front door. We went in and gave the girl at the desk my paperwork. She was gone for a few minutes. I had an uneasy feeling and told my cousin if I heard anybody mention San Bernardino, etc., I would run. When I heard someone mention a fugitive warrant, I ran down the hall, down the stairs, and across the street. As I got midway through the parking lot, several policemen drove up and surrounded me, guns out. I found myself on the ground in handcuffs again.

Again, nobody came to extradite me. I know all those years, God, somehow, continually showed me His grace. During this time, my cousin, Butch, and I broke into a liquor store. In October 1983, I went to Denver to work at the Decorating Company. The norm was to work until New Year's and then leave Colorado. I stayed longer and got a job as a cook at a restaurant. On the first day, the head waitress, Gianna, put a meal ticket up for herself. I cooked the meal and then took my break and took the meal to her.

As we sat there at the employee table, I said, "Gianna, you have beautiful eyes."

She said, "Tony, I believe God has allowed our paths to cross so I can bring you back to God."

I jokingly told her the eye thing was just a compliment. She told me at one time she was married and got hurt but was fine now. She saw that I had been hurt and was running from God and had a calling in my life.

For the next month, I went to her house a few times. She shared some experiences in her life, and we read the Bible together. I felt at ease around her and looked forward to seeing her. On February 13, 1984, after partying all weekend, I went to Gianna's apartment. I was drunk and knew she'd be up getting ready for work. I knocked on her door; she let me in. I put my arm around her, told her I loved her, and she said, "Tony, do you love yourself?" I told her I couldn't stand myself. She said if I couldn't love myself, how could I love someone else? She also said she was afraid for my life.

In the month she knew me, many of my relatives would call and tell her I had been shot at, pistol-whipped, and involved in other situations. She said, "Tony, we're going to find you dead in some alley one day. You need God in your life."

I told her I was leaving. I walked out and decided to commit suicide.

I had a plan. At 5:00 a.m., I was walking in the snow to play God and take my life. As I walked, I cried, thinking about how messed up my life was. Everything Gianna had said kept playing in my mind. I turned the corner on 38th and Federal and saw a sign in the window of a storefront church: "Jesus loves you and so do we, Victory Outreach." I stood there for a minute. It was like the floodgates opened, and I cried like I've never cried before.

A young man came out of that storefront church (Pepe Gonzales, now a Pastor of Victory Outreach, Reno Nevada) and said God had spoken to him the night before and told him to go to church and pray. He had been praying all night, and he had just looked up and seen me standing there crying. He told me they had just opened up a home and I would be the first one to come in.

I went into the home. A few weeks later, an evangelist was coming to speak at the church, so we went out with fliers to invite people. Three times we went past where Gianna lived, and her car wasn't there. I stopped one day and knocked on the door; someone answered and said they didn't know Gianna. I thought about Gianna a lot. I felt she played a big part in the last month of my life, like a real angel sent from God.

On the last night of the revival, I was sitting in the front row of the church, where the people from the home sat. I looked around as I did every night, hoping to see Gianna. I spotted her in the back row. She smiled a big smile, tears coming down her cheeks, and she waved. I was so happy to see her. She came up after the service and asked if she could speak to me, but she was told she couldn't because of the rules of the home. She turned and walked away. We waved goodbye to each other, and I never saw Gianna again. I looked for her a few times, but she had disappeared. An angel? I don't know!

All my life, I rebelled against authority. Nobody could tell me what to do. Now I was in a home with three staff members, the pastor, and his wife. I felt there were too many chiefs and not enough Indians. But God was good. He pulled me out of a deep, deep pit. I was so tired of living life on the run. Brother Pepe Gonzales was the youngest on staff. He came from California with Pastor Bobby and Sister Margie. They all had a big part in what God wanted to do in my life. Pepe (who would one day become a pastor) was a big help to me. Thank you, Pastor Pepe.

I felt out of place. I'd disappeared from the radar; nobody knew where I was. But it was too hard for me to be in the home in this environment. On Cinco de Mayo, my mother came to Colorado from Vegas, and I thought I was ready to leave the home. I went back to Vegas. The night I got back, I thought I'd take a walk and went into a bar. The next thing I knew, I woke up in my mother's house, with blood all over me, and didn't even know what had happened. I searched every place for a wound; my front tooth had been knocked out.

I knew I had to leave Vegas. My grandmother, Margaret Pacheco, called from Union City California and said, "Mijo, when are you going to come to visit?" I soon purchased a ticket and flew to California.

In her apartment complex were some property maintenance guys who were heroin addicts. I started shooting heroin and partying with them. I got a job cooking on a catering truck making some decent money. This was the last fling.

A woman named Anita lived in the apartments. Her mother had been a friend of all my aunts for many years. She had heard cassette tapes of me preaching when I was an evangelist. She had heard I was in a Victory Outreach in Denver and wondered if it was the same Victory Outreach from Hayward. She invited me to church, where Pastor Steve Pineda and Sister Josie were the pastors. Pastor Steve advised me to go into the home in San Francisco, and they would go to court with me to have me court-ordered into the home.

I told him I would take care of the nationwide fugitive warrant on my own and then go into the home. Anita and her family took me all over the Bay Area, showing me practically everything there was to see. One day, I spoke to a relative on the phone from Oakland who I hadn't seen since I was five years old. He invited me to Oakland, so I took the BART train on a Friday. We drank tequila all day Friday and Saturday, and on Sunday, we walked all over

Mission Blvd. I told him I wanted to go back to his house because of the warrant.

As we were walking, the moment I knew would one day come was upon me. The police rolled up on us and asked for IDs. I was drunk and didn't know where I was, but I knew this time I would finally have to "pay the piper." I knew I wouldn't see the light of day for many, many years. Once again, I was in those cold, cold handcuffs, waiting for the ID check. No way around this one.

I was busted. Do not pass go... Go directly to jail and then to prison. My days of running from the law were over. I felt some relief, but I wasn't looking forward to the time. I was booked in North County Oakland and was told that San Bernardino had forty days to extradite me.

I've heard that one a few times through the years. Could it be another one of those times the ball was dropped, or the paperwork got misplaced, or the time expired, or whatever God did in the past? Forty days to wait in North County Oakland—why couldn't they just send a transport right now? I was as ready as I'd ever be. I always knew I would make it to prison—here I go!

On the fortieth day, I asked, "What happens if they don't come?

They said, "They have until noon today. If they're not here by noon, we'll release you!"

I was like a lion pacing the cell, anticipating, praying, nervous, sweating, and anxious.

Ten minutes before noon, I made a phone call: "I'll be out in a few minutes; I'll meet you." I hung up the phone, excited and ready to go.

"Huereña," I heard, "roll it up."

I walked out into the walkway to be met with shackles and handcuffs.

"San Bernardino's here."

The Grey Goose picked me up, and we went to San Quentin. I spent the night there. *So this is what the next fifteen years or so of my life will be like*, I thought. I figured I better get used to it. The next day, we were on our way to San Bernardino, California. I knew one day I had to go.

I was in the processing tank, waiting, waiting, waiting. I thought, *Now these guys sure are slow to get me into new clothes and into the cell. I just want to sleep.* A bailiff came to the tank. That's right, a bailiff!

He said, "Today's your lucky day.

I said, "Lucky? I'm facing twenty-five years or more. What do you mean lucky?"

"In the years you've been running, one of the witnesses in your case has deceased and one is a mental institution. We have no witnesses. In a few minutes, you're going to stand before a judge. He will tell you your case is dismissed and order you to leave the state of California."

CHAPTER IV

THE ASSIGNMENT OF SEEING THE HEART

The Heart of Broken People (1984-1991)

God brought broken and lost men, and I raised up staff, head staff, and directors. They were broken vessels, about to be prepared for their master's use.

Wow! Leave California, not! I went back to the Bay Area and went into the Victory Outreach home in San Francisco. Gilbert Alcala was the pastor, Louie Duran was the director, and Harvey was the head staff—and he openly admitted he didn't like me. He tried everything to make it hard on me, but God was using iron to sharpen iron. Louie Duran (soon-to-be pastor) said, "Tony, from what you've told me, you've always had a problem with authority. God has placed Harvey here to teach you to submit to authority."

From sunup to sundown, Harvey rode me. He became my thorn in the flesh. Anita came to visit and would put money on my books at the home. She had three children, Stephanie, Celestino, and Shauna.

One night, I was in the prayer closet asking God to take me out of the home or take Harvey out of the home. God spoke to me and said, "Harvey is packing his clothes and is ready to leave. Go to his door and tell him I said not to leave. If he leaves, he will die of an overdose."

I said, "Lord, I don't want to go tell him not to leave, I want him to leave."

"What's more important—your comfort or Harvey's soul?"

I went to Harvey's door and knocked.

Harvey looked out the door and said, "What do you want, stupid?"

"The Lord told me you are packing and getting ready to leave the home. He said if you leave, you will die of an overdose."

"God said this to you?"

"Yes."

I could see his suitcases on the bed. Harvey did not leave then, and his attitude changed from that day forward. Sometime later, Harvey left and died of an overdose.

I left the home and went back to Hayward, married Anita, and raised Celestino, Stephanie, and Shauna for eight years. I started going to computer college and teaching at the home there. My pastor, Steve Pineda, asked me to direct the home. I wanted to finish computer college and be a computerized office specialist. I told Pastor Steve to let me finish school and we'll see. I really did not want to direct a home. Pastor Dominic and I went horseback riding almost every Saturday. And every time we rode, Dominic asked if I would run the home. He'd say, "You know you're called to run a home."

During the last month of the computer course, the registrar of the college called me into the office and said, "Tony, I have watched you every day. I have seen you come in an hour early and stay an hour later. You are one of the top in your class. I have a friend at Chevron Corporation in Richmond, California who owes me some favors. I could get you a job. All you have to do is show up—no test, just start working. Your job would be to communicate with people in the OPEC countries."

I told him I was interested, and I was set to start the Monday after Valentine's Day.

While I was attending school, I continued teaching at the house and volunteering at Trinity broadcast. The Saturday before I was to start working at Chevron, Pastor Dominic asked again if I would direct the home. I said, "Pastor, I am going to start working at Chevron Corporation Monday; they're starting me at $2,500 a month." As soon as I said that, my horse went wild, ran down the steep hill, and came to a stop. I flew over the horse, landed on my thumb, and broke the vernacular bone in my right hand.

Suddenly, I could relate to Saul of Tarsus on his way to Damascus, except my eyes were opened that day. I told Pastor Dominic I would probably run the home. It's amazing how God works things out the way He wants them to go.

I thank God for His amazing grace. Why He would consider me to be the one to run this home, I'll never know! I would be under Pastor Steve (RIP), one of the best pastors ever. Pastor Al Loma was the assistant pastor. He and Sister Debbie are my friends even to this day.

This was the beginning of the journey of which God spoke to me at the recycling plant, "to see the hearts of people." When I took over the home, three guys lived there. I knew we would need a bigger house. Then the owner said we needed to move; he was selling the house. During the month we had to move, the home grew to forty guys and a family.

One day, the driver and I were in the van looking for a home. I told him to keep an eye open for any "For Rent" signs. I fell asleep, and when I woke up a few minutes later, we were at a stop sign. I looked around to figure out where we were, and across the street, I spotted a paper on an office window. We drove a few blocks, and I told the driver to turn around and go back to that building. We pulled up behind it and I saw a five-bedroom house attached to the office building.

I called the phone number. I told the guy there would be drug addicts, alcoholics, and guys coming from prison. God changed some of their lives and they, in turn, would help others.

The property owner said, "I don't care what you use it for. I don't believe in God; I'm an atheist. As long as your money is green, that's all I care about. On the first of every month, I will be there to collect, and I expect the money to be ready."

I met with him and told him, "A fool says in his heart there is no God. One day you will know the power of Jesus Christ and you will know there's a God. One day you'll ask for God's help."

God had begun to bring in broken and lost men. Victory Outreach was about to send their first international church to Amsterdam Holland. I wanted these men to catch the vision. We prayed for South Africa, Amsterdam, the Philippines, and many other places. I raised up staff, head staff, and assistant directors. Some of these guys were broken vessels, about to be prepared for their Master's use. Thank you, Lord, for bringing in men like Richard, Danny, Phillip, Chuck, Frankie, Larry, Francisco, and many more.

Some of these guys came in kicking heroin. We literally stayed up all night with some of them and prayed until God healed them. Some came in very sick. One came in with full-blown AIDS. God showed me their hearts. They became servants and warriors, and some of them were very humble.

Many of these men were changed drastically and had a heart after God. Victory Outreach had about ten homes in Northern California. My heart was on evangelism. I caught my pastor's vision and wanted to instill it into the hearts of the men God sent to me.

I started what I called "The Northern Kingdom for Christ." All the homes in Northern California took turns going to each home, and we would take the gospel to the streets, into some of the neighborhoods that the police didn't even want to go to. We would even snatch men and women from these neighborhoods and take them to the homes.

Pastor Albert Loma, along with Dominic, Bob, Ronnie, and Herman, got a band together, Victory Outreach Band of Haywood. Pastor Steve had a great heart for the streets. The band would play in Oakland, Haywood, Union City, and all over. We had street rallies and gang rallies and did some damage to Satan's kingdom.

I showed these guys how to teach and pray, and we constantly went out to save souls. These were some very trying times having forty men in the home at any given time, and a family. But God is good.

The property owner came for the rent on the first of the month. It seemed like every time he came, we were in Bible study, and he would sit quietly and listen. God was doing something to this man. I had eight staff in the home, a head of staff, and an assistant director. It was beautiful to see these men come in broken and to see the growth right before my eyes. They became humble servants, pastors, and evangelists.

One night I took a few of them to Nations Burgers after a church service. As we stood in line along the wall, a fight broke out between some Northeno and Sureno gang members. Both gangs originated in the prison system. Northeno gang members were from northern California, and Sureno gang members were from southern California.

We were trying to calm the guys down. One guy went out the front door; many people were hiding under tables. I went out the back door of the restaurant and came to the front just as the guy drove his car up to the front door. He went to his trunk and pulled out a shotgun. I reached him and told him that Jesus loved him. I ministered to him for a few minutes and tears came down his cheeks. He put the gun back and his gang left. Thank you, Jesus.

Miracles were a daily occurrence. One night, I was in my study down in the basement and heard a knock on my door. It was the property owner, the atheist. He appeared to be scared—shaking and nervous. I asked him what was wrong. He said he had somebody in the car and didn't know what was wrong or what to do with her. He needed my help.

I said, "My help or God's help?"

I told him to bring her in. She came in and she was high on crack and demon-possessed. I told him he definitely needed God's help and asked him to go to his truck and wait. I called a few guys downstairs, and we laid hands on her and prayed in the name of Jesus. She was set free. He came back in and was amazed at the difference in her. We prayed for him.

While I was director there, Nicky Cruz, a very good friend of Pastor Sonny Arguinzoni and Pastor Steve, came to the Bay Area a lot and we got to know him and do rallies with him. Soon after the issue with the demon-possessed girl, the owner told us he was selling the property and we had to leave in sixty days.

I prayed and said, "Abba Father, I never asked you for anything for myself, but in the next place we get, I want three things: A horse I can ride anytime I want, a big fireplace, and an office designed in all Denver Bronco's colors (only because we were in Oakland Raiders territory).

We desperately needed a van for the home; all we had was a truck. One day I told the guys we would pray for a van, and we were all on one accord. Later the head staff said, "I think you'll want to take this phone call."

An older woman on the phone asked if I was the director, and I told her I was. She said she was praying and had a flyer from our home next to her, and God told her we needed a van. She asked if this was correct. I told her we were just praying for a van.

She said her husband had passed away five years prior and he had a van in which he had put new upholstery, a new engine, a new transmission, tires, and it had a new paint job. It had been up for sale for a year, but God told her to give it to us. She asked if we wanted it. I said yes and we picked it up. God is good.

We were looking for a place to move the home to, and some guy told us about a fifty-acre ranch six miles up a canyon road in the Hills. He said it jokingly as if to say we couldn't afford it. I told him, "My God owns cattle on a thousand hills, and He'd kill one for us." I went to look at it. This fifty-acre ranch had one horse (which was given to me with all the food I needed to feed him), a huge fireplace, and a big office designed in Denver Bronco colors.

About three days after we moved in, somebody put a covered wagon on the side of the road at the beginning of Canyon Road. On the wagon, they put a huge, furry, black gorilla with a rifle in his hands. I thought that was strange. Who would do anything like that?

A few days later, I had the van full of guys with me, and most of them were big boys from around the Oakland area. A truck full of guys pulled up, and one guy got out. I got out of the van.

He said, "Did you see the wagon and gorilla down there?"

I told him I was wondering who would do something like that. He said the Canyon was all Ku Klux Klan and we weren't wanted there. I told him God put us here and only God would take us out, and that no weapon formed against us could prosper. His guys got out of the truck, and the guys in the van got out, and I told him how big our God is. They told us to leave the canyon. I assured them, "We will when God says so!" We never had another problem with them. Thank you, Lord.

About this time, I was asked to go to Amsterdam, Holland to run the training center for Europe. My job was to take guys from the US to the streets of the countries in Europe and train them in evangelism. I wanted to do this so badly. Anita and I were fighting constantly, and she didn't want to go to Amsterdam.

About this time, my daughter, who I hadn't seen since she was two years old (because her mother refused to let her see me), reached out to me. She was now seventeen years old. Anita and I started fighting and arguing over my daughter. I felt I had raised her children (whom I loved very much for eight years) and there shouldn't be an issue concerning my daughter. Things continued to get worse, and I grew disheartened.

I went to San Francisco to get away for a day, and the devil really worked on me. I ended up in bed with a woman. I was ashamed, frustrated, and felt so all alone. I had blown it and felt it was the end of my life. I really had no idea what to do. I told Pastor Steve I was stepping down from the ministry. He asked why and I told him I committed adultery. He was so understanding and told me everything would be okay and that God still loved me. He said I shouldn't step down. They still wanted me to go to Amsterdam, but I knew there was something in my heart and I couldn't forget about it. I needed to deal with it.

So all these years, not only was God showing me the hearts of the guys coming into the home, but now I had to search my own heart and allow God to do some work there. I felt so much guilt and shame; I just couldn't get over it. Between arguing with Anita, the shame, and the desire to see my daughter, everything got the best of me. I decided to go to Colorado to be near my daughter.

CHAPTER V
THE HEART OF GANG MEMBERS (1991-1999)

Nicky Cruz's son-in-law, Patrick Dow, his wife Alicia, Luis Cortez, and I sat there at a table in a meeting room of a Catholic Church in Colorado Springs, along with all the O.G.s of all the gangs in the city. The tension was so thick you could cut through it with a butter knife. We started with prayer. We needed God, and there was nothing we could do. Only God could do this.

I got to Colorado just in time for Linda's seventeenth birthday. It was so nice to see my daughter after not seeing her for fifteen years. I ran into an old homeboy who was working at a detox center. I applied and got the job as a Detox Specialist. My job was to drive to Walsenburg and Trinidad on the graveyard shift to transport those who were intoxicated and had been arrested. I was to wake them up in their holding cells and tell them I would transport them to detox. They would be there for three to five days.

Some of them were cooperative and some not so cooperative. I was to take them to detox with no restraints. Some of them were violent and had to be forced into the vehicle. I had come to Colorado with the desire to open my own rehab home, agency, or program. What did I know about opening an agency? I didn't know where to go, how to start, or what to do. All I knew was I wanted to continue helping people. This began my career as a counselor. I took classes and training in the field of drug/alcohol counseling.

I spent a lot of time with my daughter. It felt great to establish a relationship with her. I moved to Colorado Springs after a few months and worked at a drug alcohol agency. I started as a part-time UA tech. After a few weeks, the Certified Addiction Counselor (C.A.C) III resigned. The owner of the agency asked if I would consider taking the classes to become a C.A.C. III. She would pay for all the classes to fast track me. I accepted.

I saw the signs of gang activity and graffiti popping up everywhere and began communicating with the police chief, city council, and the mayor. I mentioned the problem I was seeing and, of course, they responded, "There is no problem in our city that the police can't handle." Soon the violence, shootings, and killings began. Every day, articles appeared in the newspaper. So I considered opening a home for at-risk youth, specifically gang-affiliated youth.

God dealt with me on a daily basis. I put together a business plan, a program outline, the rules and regulations of the program, and went out with a proposal to open this home and fulfill my next assignment. The program "Unida" was birthed. I spoke to judges and the Department of Social Services and went to visit every youth program I could find.

A reporter for Channel 13 somehow heard about what I was trying to do to help curb the youth violence and asked if she could interview me. I did the first interview, and she was very impressed with my knowledge about gangs, which was all new to Colorado.

Later, a deaf/mute fourteen-year-old girl was coming out of a building downtown. She saw a friend across the street and began communicating through sign language. A car full of gang members drove up and shot her point-blank in the face and killed her. Her mother had seen my interview and called the station to obtain my contact information. She asked if I would consider spearheading a vigil in memory of her daughter. I didn't know exactly what that would entail, but I agreed. I rallied the community, churches, businesses, programs, city officials, and everyone I could. Soon it was known as the thirteen weeks of Stop the Violence.

I met a guy who would become one of my best friends, Luis Cortez (rest in peace, my brother). His organization, the WaysOut Program, was geared toward helping gang-affiliated youth make the right choices and obtain an education. Luis introduced me to many of these gang members, and I found out many of them were O.G.s (Original Gangsters or leaders) of some of the gangs in Colorado Springs. I realized I was taking on more than I could handle on my own. I really needed God for what I was about to get into.

Luis and I started facilitating four- and eight-hour workshops and classes on gang awareness. I was soon a certified trainer for the State and went around training police officials, teachers, foster parents, counselors, etc. Luis had gotten a $3,000 grant for a special project for one of his students. The student left the program and donated the money for a paperback autobiography I had been writing. Soon, *Busted, Disgusted, and Couldn't Be Trusted* was published. I distributed the book in all the classes I taught, in the jail, detention centers, and every place I could.

I continued taking the classes required to obtain the C.A.C. III license and working on the gang issue. Albert and Debbie Loma had just come from California to start a Victory Outreach church in Colorado Springs. Nicky Cruz's outreach, "Truce," was about to start. I asked Nicky's son-in-law, Patrick, and his daughter, Alicia, to help me and the WaysOut Program create a peace treaty among the gangs. They accepted and we began the process. I had found out that gangs from Chicago, California, Denver, and Albuquerque were in the midst of an all-out war to control all the cities along I-25 and I-70 and move the drugs along the corridors. All the gangs were recruiting in grade schools, middle schools, and high schools. There were gang-related shootings and killings weekly, and, finally, the city officials and police department realized the city was experiencing a major problem. They needed help and, believe me, they needed more than we could do. They needed God! Albert Loma starting the church, Nicky's Truce, and the thirteen weeks of Stop the Violence all happened at the same time. God is the Master

Coordinator. Even Stevie Wonder could see God was moving. Behind the scenes, God was about to perform a city-wide miracle.

I met with the mayor and city council to make a proposal. I told them in return for a peace treaty, the gangs would probably want something. I absolutely had no idea what I was doing. I had never read a manual on how to create a peace treaty nor did I have instructions. I know this had to be God and God alone. All these years I had admired David Wilkerson for the gang rally he did in New York. God used that just for Nicky Cruz. All the street rallies we did in California, all the training and preparation in East L.A., San Francisco, Hayward, and all the other cities—I thank God He knows what to do.

The mayor and city council promised to do whatever it took if we worked out the peace treaty. We needed a safe place to meet with the O.G.s, and the priest of St. Joseph's Church in South Gate opened the door for us. Patrick Dow, Alicia, Luis Cortez, and I met the O.G.s there. The tension was so thick you could cut through it with a butter knife. We started with prayer. We needed God; there was nothing we could do—only God could do this. The first meeting went well, and we met a few times and worked out the peace treaty.

In return for peace, the gangs wanted a gym and other things to do in the community. We went back to the mayor and city council to hold them to their promise. They assured us they would come through. Soon, the police took all the information we got and started coming down hard on gang members. We were deceived.

Nicky Cruz's outreach, the WaysOut Program, and Unida washed their hands of the situation. But thank God, the peace held up. It appeared everything fell apart, but when God does something, He does it right!

Because of the gang violence, Unida was a rare commodity. Rita (the owner of the drug/alcohol agency I was working for) asked if I would allow Unida to be under the umbrella of her program. She saw it as a moneymaker. I told her I wouldn't do that because she wouldn't know how to help youth in gangs. She demanded I just focus on the agency or leave. By this time, God had brought certain people into my life who would push me into my assignment. Judge Regina embraced Unida and appreciated what Nicky, Patrick, Alicia, Luis, and I had done to stop the violence. She would play an important part in my life for many years to come. So I left the agency, not knowing what was next. I was asked to do in-house training for a large agency that had several homes in the state of Colorado. I facilitated an eight-hour workshop for all the employees.

After the class was over, the two co-owners made me an offer I couldn't turn down, especially since I was now unemployed. But God knows how to lead us where He wants us to go! I had mentioned in the class that my years of experience led me to open a specialized home for gang-affiliated youth. Their proposal was to take over one of the homes being closed by the state and get it back in good standing. They would allow Unida to be under their 501c3 non-profit organization and I would be independent, with no strings attached. I told them I would, under one condition, that

I could do it with little or no restrictions from the company. They agreed. I set out to get this home up and running again and found total chaos. The staff members were having orgies in the home after the teens were in bed, one of the staff was performing sexual favors for some of the teens, and another was teaching them to worship Satan. There was no order, discipline, or structure whatsoever. All the carpet had been taken off and rolled up along walls and stairs; it desperately needed paint, and holes were everywhere. What did I get myself into? Talk about fighting a spiritual battle!

I walked into the house and fired everyone (strike one), hired my childhood homeboy, who was now C.A.C. certified, and hired a few other people who had lived a rough life and whose lives had changed (strike two). I also hired an assistant manager who had been a drug addict in the past and was now a counselor (strike three). I found out that Judge Regina was the judge getting ready to close the home down; she was now over the juvenile court. I called her to let her know I was running the home now and to ask her to give me a chance to get it in order. She agreed and said I should inform her if I ever left the position. We got the place looking good, put a structure in place, and began to teach the teens discipline. The police department and social services visited the home and were very impressed with the changes both in the home and in the teens. Social services referred teens, but I didn't allow it to be a dumping ground for just everyone.

One day I received a call from the owners to attend a mandatory meeting at the main office in Colorado Springs. I walked into the room and the owners were at one end of the table, surrounded by several others I had never met. An open seat at the other end of the table had been saved just for me. I felt like I was invited to lunch and I was the main course. The owners asked if I had ever met Francine, who was sitting next to me. I said no.

They said Francine would be taking over the home and asked me to give a thirty-day resignation because I should have hired better people, with a master's degree. They didn't approve of the past lifestyles of the guys I hired. I asked if a master's degree was a prerequisite. They said yes. I asked them if they knew my past and that all I had was a high school diploma. They looked at me as if they were shocked and asked for a thirty-day resignation again. I thought for a moment and decided to quit that day. I said, "Thank you, but before I leave, I need to make a phone call." I dialed Judge Regina's cell phone number. To my surprise, Regina answered the phone. I made sure they knew to whom I was speaking. I told Regina, "As of today, I am no longer running the home." She thanked me. Within a few months, all the agency's homes were closed down.

Not really knowing what to do, where to go, and questioning if I had missed God, someone mentioned trying to get a home opened in Walsenburg, Colorado. I went to the police department, sheriff's office, and probation department. The sheriff was a Christian and said he wanted me to meet Judge Appel. We walked over to the courthouse and the court clerk took us into the judge's chamber. I showed Judge Appel the proposal for a home for gang-affiliated youth. He was so excited. He suggested we open as a Specialized Group Home under the umbrella of the Department of Social Services and Department of Probation. And get this, we would get paid! Judge Appel said, "You get a house and I'll fill it up."

I got a job and started Unida Youth Outreach. We met in a church. Pretty soon, the groups were full, and I saw a lot of graffiti all over town (not again)! Yes, you guessed it, the same thing was happening in Walsenburg that happened in Colorado Springs a year before. I started the process again, meeting with the police chief, mayor, city council, etc.

I heard the same story, "We don't have a problem we can't deal with." I met with the high school principal to see about meeting with some of the known gang members in the school. I got the same response, "We don't have a gang problem." Within a few weeks, I received a phone call from the principal and the police chief asking for some advice. I met with the gang members in the schools, inquiring about the O.G.s. It wasn't long before we were working on the peace treaty.

I received a phone call from someone saying he had heard we were looking for side jobs to get a house for the program. He told me about a doctor in town who needed help moving out of a rental, and the house might be right for what we had in mind. I went to help move the doctor. The house was a five-bedroom and had a duplex in the back. I asked for the owner's phone number. I called Tony and told him what I wanted to do with the house and that we didn't have a deposit or the full rent. We were going on the word of Judge Appel that he would fill the home up. But, most importantly, I knew this was nothing short of the will of God. Tony told me to take over the property— no deposit and no rent until we started generating money. God is awesome! We moved in on a Saturday; on Monday afternoon, the home was full.

Immediately, we came under attack by the neighbors. People began picketing, going to the mayor, City Hall, and the police department. Judge Appel would tell them, "Leave my baby alone." He embraced Unida and appreciated what the program was doing in and for the community. We were still working on the peace treaty, and I invited Denver Victory Outreach's drama, *Gangsta's Paradise*, to come to Walsenburg where we rented the theater. It was packed out, and many souls were saved that night. The peace treaty was a success and Walsenburg experienced peace again.

We were in the midst of a spiritual battle. The devil was hitting the home in many ways. Some people in the community had created an uproar, along with some business owners. The mayor did not like me or the idea of a home for gang members in his community. They wanted to lock these "bad kids" up and send them away. Thank God by this time Judge Appel, the police chief, and the Department of Social Services were on board and fought for us. I had never experienced the enemy's onslaught like that.

Many prominent people in high places were using and selling drugs. Some were in the police department, sheriff's department, and other entities. The police chief was a good Christian brother and got fired, another prominent man was a Christian brother and lost his job, and the pastor who allowed our youth to use the church for the meetings was asked by the Board of Directors to resign. I could see the spiritual warfare taking place on all levels.

The city council ordered a town hall meeting to see what should be done about the home and these "bad kids." Some youth were charged with smoking a joint, and they wanted to lock them up for these little things. After hearing all I could tolerate, I stood up and addressed the mayor, some city council members, and those who were part of this conspiracy to close the home down. I brought up the evil things taking place in secret and how the youth didn't have many good influences to look up to. I pulled covers on several people and confronted the mayor. The home was eventually accepted and loved by many in the community. We were blessed and highly favored. We used the five-bedroom house and the duplex as a home for males, females, and the developmentally disabled.

After eight years, a new Director of Social Services was hired, and I was told that some rules regarding prayer, church services, and discipline for the youth would have to change. They could no longer be mandatory if the program was to continue to be funded. I told him I would rather close the home than to change the rules and structure of the program and that the money was not the reason the home was open. If God would be taken out of the homes, the home had no reason to exist.

J.D. Curry was the district manager for the southern part of American National Insurance in Colorado. Every time he was in

Walsenburg to recruit an insurance agent, he would invite me to lunch. For months he tried to get me into the insurance field, and for months I wanted nothing to do with it. Jim was persistent and we became friends. I told him I knew nothing about insurance, and I didn't know if I'd be a good salesman. He assured me that I had what it took to be productive. The pay would start at $500.00 a week, and I would be on commission after I got licensed. I felt I had fulfilled the assignment at hand, so I took the job. I took all the state tests to be an insurance agent and began working.

CHAPTER VI

THE HEART OF THE CORPORATE WORLD (1999-2002)

The Field Director, the CEO of the Insurance Company, and I sat there in the sitting room of a five-star hotel in Denver, Colorado. The CEO turned to me and said, "Tony, we want you to be careful and aware that we are dropping you off in a pool of sharks."

As part of American National Insurance, my job was to make appointments when Jim came to town every week to collect premiums from current customers.

I knew many people and was related to half the town on my mother's side of the family. I was making five to six appointments a week for Jim to show the insurance plans. While in training before I got licensed, I made $500 a week. For every sale I made, the commission was put into an account for when I got my license. All the commissions would be divided into the quarter, which is what my paycheck would be weekly.

At the first weekly district meeting, two guys sat at a table in front of me. Both of them had been working for the company for twenty-plus years. One guy I'll call Sam had been the leading agent in the district for eighteen years running. I asked him about something in the new agent's book and he replied, "I'm the leading agent in the district and I don't talk to rookies."

I said, "Thank you, congratulations, but you are the leading agent only because you never had competition. From now on, you'll see me running way up there in front of you."

The two of them laughed. Jim (the district manager) was my sales manager and another sales manager was Sam's sales manager. I didn't know this then, but the two sales managers were betting on Sam and me.

My license was held up a little longer than usual because of my past records, and, finally, my license was issued. I broke my first quarter with a weekly check of $2,000, and I still had no idea what I was doing! But it was fun, and I was the leading agent in the district. I saw that this was a dog-eat-dog environment. God was about to show me the heart of greed, immoral work ethics, lying, and cheating in the corporate world.

I thanked God daily for this opportunity, and I was really enjoying it. However, I attracted enemies because I was the leading agent. In this environment, one could easily be swayed by mammon's enticing lure. I knew that this era would be short-lived. The money was good, but this wasn't me, and I knew it. Many of the people I showed the insurance plans to were living on a very limited income, and I couldn't see trying to sell them something they couldn't afford that would hurt their family. Other agents discussed how they got people to buy the most expensive policies so they could get points toward trips and other incentives. God was testing me so I could see what I would do—stay humble and do what is right.

I wasn't trying for the incentives and trips, but, somehow, I continued to be the leading agent in the district for the whole twenty-one months I was an agent. I could only attribute this to God. I questioned His plan for my life. What was I doing here? I saw a lot of shady things some people were doing to make money. I won trips to San Francisco and a week in a five-star hotel, all expenses paid. I was there with the top agents in the United States. I won a trip to Hawaii (I didn't go). After a year and three months of being an agent, Jim asked me to move to Pueblo for a sales manager position. I moved and waited four months, but nothing happened. I had an offer to work for another agency in Phoenix to train agents on selling life insurance. The agents in this district sat in an office waiting on phone calls, making phone calls for property/casualty, and had no idea how to sell life insurance.

I told Jim I'd wait another two months but would take the other position if nothing happened. I've always enjoyed training people. Jim was trying hard to fire the sales manager and place me in the position, but in the insurance field, it's almost impossible to fire insurance agents. I gave my resignation and waited for Jim to hire my replacement. I told Jim where I'd be working and asked him to stay in touch with me.

During the last district meeting, I made a paper crown, gave it to Sam, and told him he could be king of the agency again. I took the position in Phoenix. My pay was reduced by $1,000 a week, but I wanted out of Pueblo and I'd be more in my element. I immediately started training agents. I took a different agent out into the community daily, sold a lot of insurance, and made some money for the agents and the agency. Most of all, souls were saved. Our Father, in His infinite wisdom, was giving me fast-track training for what was about to take place next.

One morning a few months into the job, I was talking to the district manager in his office when the phone rang. Greg answered the call and handed the phone to me and said, "It's Dixie McDaniels."

Dixie was the CEO of the insurance company I was employed by a few months earlier.

"Hello," I said.

"Hello, Mr. Huereña, this is Dixie McDaniels from the Corporate Office." She said Jim had given her my phone number and that a district manager position was available in Denver. It paid $2,000 a week plus commission on everything sold by the agents. There were thirteen insurance agents, two receptionists, two sales managers, and a personal secretary. The company would pay for my move, pay for me to stay in a five-star hotel until I found a house, and pay the first six months for the house I chose.

I told her I wasn't interested.

She said, "Mr. Hiereña, you were one of the top two agents in the whole state of Colorado. The company has been around since 1905 and never in the company's history have we offered an agent this position. Usually, you must go through five years as a sales manager, but we are offering you the position. Jim spoke so highly of you and felt you are the right person for the job."

I told her again I wasn't interested. She asked me to think about it and she would call back. I reassured her I wasn't interested and said goodbye. A few days later, Dixie called again and asked me to be the district manager of northern Colorado. I told her I knew nothing about being a district manager and wasn't very good at math. I didn't feel capable of doing the job.

She assured me that I had what it took to lead a district, and I accepted. I thought to myself, *Two times this woman has called to offer the position to me; I'd hate to make a mistake and regret it later.* I checked into a hotel in Lakewood and settled in on a Saturday. Monday morning, the field director, the CEO of the company, and I met in the sitting room of the five-star hotel.

They welcomed me to Lakewood and told me we would meet every day that week, get some fast-track training, and talk about the details of the district. We met every day, and one day I was told five guys in the district were district managers at one time or another. The following Monday morning, we would have a meeting to introduce me to the district. Nobody in the district knew anything about someone coming from outside the district to take the position. Everybody knew the district manager would be announced on Monday, but they thought it would be one of them.

We met the following Monday for the last morning before I was to be the new district manager. The plan was that I would wait in the hallway until I was called to come in. The field director said, "Tony, we want you to be careful and be aware that we are dropping you off in a pool of sharks." The field manager would be there for the next month training me, and the secretary and receptionists knew a lot. I assured them after being the director of various homes, I could handle any sharks.

While waiting in the hallway, I decided to go to the men's room. As I washed my hands, someone came in and asked if I was a new agent. I said, "Yeah, something like that." He told me how much experience he had and said he felt he would be the next district manager. I felt so insignificant and unsure. I wondered what I was doing and what I was getting myself into. I was about to see another type of heart (the heart of the corporate world).

The field director came out to the hallway and said, "Okay, this is your time." I went in, sat down, and waited to be introduced. I was nervous, my hands were sweating, and I felt like backing out. I felt nauseous as I stood there before "my district," as the CEO put it. I looked at every face and saw a look of anger, unbelief, discouragement, and frustration. I had no idea why I was here, but I knew only God could have done this.

The field director stayed for a month and was gone. I soon heard complaining and backstabbing. How could they bring a rookie to manage the managers? Two of the five prior district managers took me under their wings and were my go-to guys. I appreciated them. Almost immediately, I saw a loss in premium on a weekly basis. I received phone calls from frustrated clients reporting that a family member passed away and the company was refusing to pay due to a pre-existing condition. I went out to the different agents' sections of town to investigate. I saw a pattern—people who were basically on their death bed issued an insurance policy and not able to collect. Unethical things were happening. All this was happening in six agents' areas, and I suspected they were doing something shady. I met with them and told them what I suspected. I said if I was correct, there would be repercussions. I saw them as snakes and would eventually chop their heads off, meaning I would fire them.

A few months into the job, I received calls from corporate asking what was going on in the district, why all the premium loss? I also found that a few of the agents and one sales manager were calling corporate, pretending to be clients, and speaking falsely about me. I continued to investigate in the district. Many people were letting their policies go and cashing in their cash value on the policy. Everybody I spoke to said they just couldn't afford to pay the premium any longer.

Finally, I realized the six agents were working for another insurance company, stealing clients, cashing in their policies, and switching them over to the other company. This was illegal. They were issuing policies for people who couldn't be insured, falsifying applications, and having the clients lie.

The corporate office called and said I was making waves. I was told to sweep all the issues under the carpet. I kept having to deal with families paying for insurance policies and being told they couldn't collect after the death of their loved one. Agents were doing some very unethical things to get commissions and points to win trips. I was dealing with hurting family members because of it.

I joined an agent who had a gospel band, and we began to have street rallies and saw a lot of souls saved. I finally had enough proof and evidence against the agents and the sales manager, so I fired them and stopped the loss of premium in the district. I hired new agents and started thinking it was time to move on. I told the CEO to send a replacement; I was finished here. The money was good, I helped many people, and I did the best I could. I saw a different kind of heart and knew it was time to go on to the next assignment. I had never seen so much greed, lust for money, lust for fortune, and lying and jealousy in my whole life. My replacement came and asked me to stay and be his right-hand guy. I declined and went to direct a home in Denver for a year. Then I went to Las Vegas to be near my son, mother, and family.

CHAPTER VII

THE HEART OF THE ENTERTAINERS (2002-2007)

I couldn't believe my ears. I was standing there with the Bobby Ruffin from the Drifters. He said, "Tony, I've been watching you and what you're doing with the other shows. I haven't had a manager for thirty years because all the managers have done is rip me off. I should've been rich by now. Would you consider being my manager?"

So there I was back in Las Vegas. I asked myself, *Why*? All I could think of was that I needed to spend time with my family and my son, Robert. I could never describe the feeling of being close to my son, and after all these years, I would actually have my opportunity. Thank you, Lord! And it was beautiful to spend so much time with my mother. It had been years since I had spent a significant amount of time with her. I had been away for so many years in the ministry that I had forgotten how it felt to be around family.

I couldn't even begin to understand what I was doing here, or what to do. I just knew that I was confused, down on myself, and feeling lonely. After all these years of running homes and being in the ministry, I really knew nothing else (other than the insurance company). Was there life after the ministry and the home? How do you go back to living a normal life after marriage and ministry, constantly pouring yourself into others? I felt like an old, thrown-away shoe. I felt so alone in the middle of a big city, even though I had a great support system. I didn't know where to start, but I needed God's help. I felt like Jonah—out of my environment, a fish out of water!

I went up to The Strip one day to reminisce about growing up in this city, just going down memory lane. I thought I'd never be living here again. All I knew was the lifestyle I was living the last time I lived there. I knew I would never go back. I knew the city would not support any type of home, so what to do now?

I was sitting in front of the Boardwalk Casino thinking about when I was a kid, cruising up and down The Strip in my 69' Caprice. As I sat there, I noticed this young lady talking to different couples. She appeared to be having a great time. She was laughing, joking, and enjoying herself. I watched her for about an hour. I finally went over and asked what she was doing. She said she was working. I said I would love to have a job in which I could be that happy. She said, "We're hiring!" I asked what the job consisted of. She said,

"Just take a couple inside to the woman at the desk, and if she signs them up to go to the time-share, you get paid."

Really?

I got the job as a greeter working for Vinny Sr. and Vinny Jr. I soon became their number-one greeter, and they loved that I was honest, a Christian, and clean and sober. In the time-share environment, it's rare to find honesty and sobriety. There are so many con artists and shady people, another dog-eat-dog environment. Vinny Jr. appreciated the fact that he could depend on me and soon asked if I would travel to the adjoining states to recruit couples to come to Vegas.

I took up the offer and went a few days a week. Several people didn't like the idea, but God was using this (as well as the district manager position) to show me that my ministry wasn't inside the walls of a church. God used my testimony to take me from the bottom to the top. The company I was employed by was the only company that accepted single women for a time-share. Most companies required married couples making $50,000 or more annually.

The incentives for people to go to the time-share were two show tickets and two buffet tickets. Unfortunately, many of the single women had nobody to go with. I offered my services to show these women Vegas shows, and I was a testimony to many people. I was very blessed to have access to any tickets at any time.

After a few months, I was moved to a Fremont Street location. I was at the Plaza Casino a short period of time when I met Larry.

He was one of the best impersonators/comedians in Las Vegas and asked if I would consider promoting his show. I agreed and enjoyed being around Larry. I called him the hardest working man in show business. He worked from 9 a.m. until the show ended at 10 p.m. Larry was going through a hard situation, and I prayed with him behind the stage. We had many discussions about life and his issues. He was hurting because of what was going on in his life, yet he could get up and make people laugh for an hour every night.

I met the one and only Mary Wilson, from Diana Ross & the Supremes. She was doing a lounge show at the Plaza and I talked to her occasionally. When she saw me promoting the show, she'd call me up on the stage. She would say on the mic, "Santiago, come over here and give a plug for the show." Mary was a very sweet, kind, and beautiful person. This was the beginning of the ministry with Vegas entertainers.

I met a young lady (I'll call her Samantha) who was a professional showgirl. She had been in several shows, a few small parts in movies, and some commercials. She was doing a promotion at the Plaza and was wearing an angel costume. I walked by her one day with a pair of big ears on to promote the comedy show. She asked what I was doing, and I told her I was promoting Larry's show. Samantha and I visited the little cafe in the casino and drank some hot chocolate on cold nights.

We went to shows and dinner and spent time together. I couldn't understand why someone like her wanted to be with someone like me.

She simply said, "Tony, I have been in show business for many years and around people from Vegas and Hollywood. But I have never met a gentleman that has treated me like you do. Tony, you don't drink, get high, party, or anything. You're so different; you stick out like a sore thumb. Why are you in Vegas?"

All I could say was, "I don't know."

After we stopped seeing each other, I was feeling very lonely. I had found a good church to attend. The first time I went to church, the pastor prophesied over me. One night shortly after this, I was on my way home from a show listening to a song and just sobbing. I was hurting, lonely, and desperately needing a touch from God. While I was on a major intersection at a red light, A red, heart-shaped balloon with the words "I love you" floated up directly in front of me. It stayed there until the light changed, then floated away.

Soon after, Larry moved to Fitzgerald's Casino with Steve, an Elvis impersonator. Steve had been sober for five years at this point and was very involved with his church. He and Bobby Ruffin (one of the only original Drifters alive) were sharing the showroom. I ran the showroom and ticket booths on Fremont Street, promoting and marketing for the shows. I was standing outside the casino one day when Bobby Ruffin walked up and said, "Tony, I have been watching what you've been doing for Steve and Larry. I have not had a manager in thirty years." He looked sad and continued, "Would you consider managing my 'Tribute to the Drifters' show?"

Wow! I couldn't believe my ears. I said, "Bobby, I grew up listening to your music; the Drifters have always been one of my favorite groups. I don't have to consider it; I don't feel worthy to manage your show."

Bobby and I spent a lot of time together. He told me about the many years he'd been in the entertainment business, the struggles he endured. We spoke a lot about his upbringing, family, where he was now, and where he wanted to be. One time, Bobby asked me to follow him to the mechanic to drop his car off. Afterward, I was driving him back to his place. I put a CD in and asked if he knew the vocalist. It was none other than Bobby singing "Under the Boardwalk." We drove down Las Vegas Boulevard singing to the Drifters' music. Many times, I would pray for Bobby, Steve, and Larry. Bobby accepted Jesus into his heart during this time.

A well-known show producer bought Steve's show and wanted to make it big. I was working on filling the showroom, but the producer was a typical shady, selfish, deceiving person. He hired his good friend who had a bad name in the business. I was expected to sell the tickets at full price, and this guy was selling the tickets at half price.

I confronted the producer about it, and he denied it. I got proof and met with Steve and we all had a meeting. I didn't want to stop working for Steve, so I told the producer I would continue to work only because of Steve. Fremont Street made it perfectly clear that they didn't want this guy that the producer hired. This guy was so arrogant; he would walk past me with a grin on his face. I was told that if I saw him on Fremont Street at any time to call security and he would be arrested. One day, he was standing in front of the

Fitzgerald's, and I advised him to leave. He made some sarcastic remarks, so I left and alerted security. Within a few minutes, they arrived, asked him to drop to his knees, and handcuffed him.

One day I was walking around the casino promoting the shows and a group of young ladies from Texas made their way up the escalator. I put on the big ears and said, "Wellllllll doggy! Ross Perot here guys! I'm all ears; can you hear me now?" They laughed and asked what I was doing. I told them I managed and promoted some shows. They said they had a thirty-year-old niece who was a Selena impersonator. I told them to give her my phone number. One of them said, "I'll just call her right now and you talk to her." She called "Selena." We spoke for a few minutes, and I asked her to meet me the next day at the restaurant in the Fitzgerald's, wearing a Selena outfit. She did, and I comped her to see the Drifters show. We met after the show and began to hang out and became friends.

I met Rudy Regalado the Venezuelan (RIP) whose music I also grew up with. Rudy played with the likes of the infamous Tito Puente, Carlos Santana, El Chicano, Malo, and had his own group, Chevere. I spent a lot of time with him and his wife and at his drummer's music shop. I went with him a few times to Hollywood; his producer lived behind the Hollywood sign, up in the hills overlooking the city. I had many opportunities to pray with him and his wife.

A couple bought Steve's show (I will call them William and Rita). They remodeled the showroom with fifties and sixties memorabilia, hired a whole band and backup singers, and asked me to stay and work for them. They were billionaires from Texas and owned several businesses, and they went all out to make Steve's show big.

Rita was twenty years younger than William and had very low self-esteem. William had control issues. Their marriage was in dire need of help. We were trying to figure out ways to pack the showroom out and decided to get Rita and the two backup singers to dress up as showgirls and have the band dress in all black. I walked up front with Rita, Steve (Elvis) walked behind us with the two backup singers as showgirls, and the band behind them looking like bodyguards. We would walk around the casino an hour before the show, and I'd say, "The king has entered the building." People would stop what they were doing and ask Steve for an autograph, and we'd get them to come up to the showroom. Soon the showroom was packed every night.

I counseled and prayed with William and Rita and their whole family. I spent a lot of time with them. Rita was so grateful she suggested I get my own venue and have my own production. A few blocks from the Fremont Street experience was a small restaurant called Take One Club. I worked out a deal with the owner to use the club twice a week. I wanted to bring back "dinner and a show." I had the Drifters, a comedian, and dinner. Rita offered me a guitar from the Fitzgerald's showroom owned by Carlos Santana, which had his signature on it. She suggested I use it to sell raffle tickets to the Take One Club's first show.

My dream as a teenager (when I learned we were moving to Las Vegas) about my name being in lights came true, A Huereña

Production. The owners of the casino wanted to close the showroom to make more space for gaming. Spaces for shows were becoming a thing of the past. I had a personal and up-close look at the heart of entertainers, producers, and directors.

I helped start a transportation business, and the first client was Larry, a Jewish man from New York who needed chemotherapy and radiation treatment five days a week. He was very angry at the beginning because he couldn't drive any longer. I picked him up daily, took him to his treatment, waited for him, and took him back home. A little at a time, I witnessed to Larry and shared my testimony. One day he told me a dream he had during a very hard time in his life. In his dream, a man in a white robe came to him. This man had a beautiful smile and told him everything would be fine and his son (whom Larry was worried about) would also be okay. I assured him that this man was none other than Jesus Christ, the Messiah. One day after a few weeks of spending a few hours a day with Larry, I pulled over to the curb, looked in Larry's eyes, and asked him if he was ready to accept this Jesus, the Messiah, into his heart. He repeated the sinner's prayer, and soon after, Larry went home to be with the Lord!

My assignment in Las Vegas had come to an end. I believed God was leading me back to Colorado Springs. This era of my life was a very precious time, and I will be forever grateful for the opportunity to get to know all these entertainers and their families. My heart was touched by them all. God is good!

CHAPTER VIII

HEART OF THE CLEAN AND SOBER (2007-2011)

As we were driving, I spotted a banner reading "28 + bedrooms for rent." I asked Sam, "What could we do with 28 + bedrooms?"

I returned to Colorado Springs, Colorado and immediately started taking classes to reinstate my C.A.C. III. I was told I had to start the process all over again, so I decided against this option. I knew I would start a new program, but what kind? I prayed and, in the meantime, I met with the police department, mayor, Department of Social Services, probation, parole departments, and other entities.

I went to the courthouse to talk to the judges and asked questions. "What is the greatest need in the community?" "What type of home would be beneficial?" The consensus was a Clean and Sober Home. "What is a clean and sober home?" I asked, and they gave me a brief description. I did my homework and put a business plan and program outline together, and then I went out with my proposal.

Many entities said if I could get one going, I would be eligible for the monies allocated for this type of home. I went back to the courthouse to see the judge in charge of drug and alcohol cases. To my surprise, it happened to be no other than Judge Regina. When God orchestrates something, He works out every detail. Regina always appreciated what we've done in the community.

I met with Regina in her chamber. We caught up on the years and she was excited about the opportunity at hand. She said, "Find a place and I'll send people to you." I went out looking for a place in every part of the city and found a duplex in the south end of town. The owner's son was in the house. I told him what I wanted to use the duplex for, and he was very interested. I told him I didn't have the finances to start with. He said we could work something out.

I signed a contract and was told we could move in on April 1 (two weeks away). I went out looking for furniture, and God opened the door for the whole home to be fully furnished. [Thank you, Lord!] I asked my old friend, Pastor Sam, to help me move the furniture to the home. On April 1, Sam and I picked up the U-Haul truck and the furniture; it was move-in day! We got to the duplex and found a guy painting. We had agreed we would paint as per our agreement, so I asked why he was painting.

He said, "I have some bad news. My father doesn't want the duplex used for the purpose you want to use it for."

I said, "You're kidding me, right?"

He wasn't kidding. We witnessed to him, said the sinner's prayer with him, and told him not to feel bad about being unable to make this happen. I assured him God had something bigger and better in store for us.

I asked Sam if we could put the furniture in his garage for now, and he agreed. As we drove to Sam's house, we saw a banner that read "28 + bedrooms for rent." I said, "What could we do with 28 + bedrooms?" We pulled into the driveway, knocked on the door, and asked for the owner. Francesco wasn't in but would be given our phone number. I was excited and thanked God for the property.

Francesco called me a few hours later, and we made an appointment to meet. After a tour of the fifteen bedrooms and the other houses on the property, we sat there in the kitchen and told Francesco what we wanted to use the property for. He mentioned a program was looking at the property to use it for a drug/alcohol agency. I shared my testimony with Francesco—all that God had done in my life and the lives that have been changed throughout the years in the homes. I then told him I believed God allowed our paths to cross for a purpose not known to us. I found out Francesco had bought the property in October, and I arrived in Colorado Springs in October looking for the place God had in store for me next.

I told him I didn't think that was a coincidence, that this was the providence of God. He said, "I don't know about this God stuff." I assured him that he would see the hand of God, see the changes in the lives of men, and know God is real. I then laid my hands on him and prayed for him.

As we sat there talking, there was a knock on the door. It was two men from the agency interested in leasing the property. They told Francesco they had a check and had added an additional $500 to the agreed price. Francesco told them he wasn't interested in leasing the property to them and that he had just leased it to us. Sam and I looked at each other, looked up, and said, "Thank you, Lord!" Francesco said he really liked what I had done in the past and was impressed. He knew I didn't have money to get started and proposed that if I got some of the guys in the home to help remodel the place, he would give us free rent until money started coming in.

I'd like to talk about the best thing that ever happened in my life. I mentioned earlier my Aunt Lilian who was adopted by my great-grandmother. Her daughter Sally had a daughter named Carolina, who has always been very special to me. Throughout the years, I saw a heavy calling in her life, and we have always been close. I always admired her heart. We were always there for each other throughout the years. Just as this property was made available to the program, Carolina was raped and left for dead. At the same time, she was experiencing some minor issues with the courts and was ready to allow God to do whatever He wanted in her life. I opened the Women's Home for her, and we decided to get married.

Unida International Clean and Sober Home was now open. I went to the city and applied for a Conditional Use Permit (a permit allowing for more than five people to reside in the same house). I was granted one. Our neighborhood was composed of some people who were in the Ku Klux Klan and was a very tight-knit neighborhood. These people came around the property taking pictures and taking notes.

They went to the city, voiced their concerns, and fought to get us out of the neighborhood. An elderly couple who lived three houses down threatened in every way possible. We found out they had become ill. He had triple bypass surgery, and she got cancer. Carolina and I went to the couple's home to let them know Jesus loved them and so did we, and if they needed anything to just let us know. They were very angry and didn't want to talk to us.

The court, parole departments, and probation department were sending people to the home. The fifteen bedrooms on the property were full. Never once did we pay rent, utilities, or anything else. The Clean and Sober Home was a totally different type of home. Never had we received rent from anyone in the homes. Francesco taught me how to be business-minded and at the same time fulfill God's plan. Many of those in the home were out of prison, trying to work and be responsible. I saw a major difference in the quality of people in the home compared to years past. Seldom did we see any appreciation, and we heard nothing but complaining.

Francesco cooked breakfast every morning, and he and I would sit down and talk. He was a self-made millionaire and was a good friend. He saw miracles; he experienced God moving throughout the whole time we were there. Francesco offered to buy restaurants and other ventures for us to help us become successful. We appreciate everything Francesco did for us, and to this day, we still communicate with him.

After a year and a half of the neighborhood fighting against us, Carolina and I decided to go to Indianapolis. We turned the home back over to Francesco and went to Denver to spend time with our family before leaving for Indianapolis.

CHAPTER IX

HEART OF THE HOMELESS (2012-2015)

Unida International House of Restoration was now open. And things were moving quickly, so fast I couldn't keep up. God never ceases to amaze me. When God is in it, everything goes smoothly.

My wife and I stayed in Denver for a month, and then we were off to Indianapolis to visit our daughter, Linda, son-in-law, Robert, and the grandkids. We weren't thinking about starting up a new program. Basically, we were finished with homes. It was time to retire.

Robert came to Denver to help us move our belongings. We cleared a little space for Carolina to sleep, and I jokingly said by the time we got to Indianapolis, some of the things would be on top of her. Robert was driving, and we drove straight through. At 4:30

a.m., we started coming up a hill, traveling at seventy-five miles per hour. In the distance, I thought I saw something in the middle of the highway. Two semitrailers blocked both lanes and neither had their lights on. I told Robert the trucks were there.

Robert knew if he slammed on the brakes, we would rear-end one of the trucks. We swerved to the right and didn't know there was a ravine. We went down the ravine, bouncing off the huge boulders for what seemed like a never-ending period. We came to a stop at the top of the ravine on the opposite side.

All four tires were flat, the airbags popped out, and the alarm blared consistently. I immediately looked in the back where my beautiful wife was sleeping and quite a bit of our belongings had fallen on top of her. She woke up and didn't even realize what had just happened.

We got out of the van and noticed right ahead of us were two vehicles that had gone down the ravine; they had rolled and the cars were destroyed. The semitrailers had stopped to help those in the cars.

Some highway patrols came to check on us. We were a little dizzy, but we were okay. [Thank you, Lord.] I told my wife we were in God's perfect will because the devil had been at the city limits of Indianapolis, waiting to take us out. He hit us with his best shot. As I looked at the cars ahead of us and looked at our vehicle, all I could think was that the angels were there and brought us through safely. Robert called his friend to tow the vehicle. I didn't know what God was about to do, but I knew He was up to something.

Robert and our daughter, Linda, were in the ministry at Robert's uncle's church. During one service, a woman came up to us. She knew we had a home in Colorado and told us about a young lady who was in a bad situation. She asked if my wife and I would meet her and do something to help her. Raj's mother, Surinder, came to meet us at our daughter's house. She was very concerned about her daughter and wanted to see if we could help her. We told her we'd be happy to see what we can do.

We prayed with Raj, and she said she wanted help. My wife told her we wouldn't help until she went to the doctor to see what was wrong with her. She had a problem with drinking and looked very sick. Raj went to the emergency room and was told had she not gone, she could have died. During the month she was in the hospital, Raj called us daily asking if we would help her.

I didn't want to open another home, especially a home for women. Living in a home for women is not easy to do. But my wife is very sensitive to the Spirit of God and has a soft heart. She immediately asked if we could get a place just to help Raj. Since my wife and I have been together, I have always prayed and asked God to have my wife be part of the decision if He is leading us in a certain direction. I want her to say that God has put it in her heart. I agreed to get a place to open a home for Raj.

Within a few days, Robert and Linda told us that Victor (a guy Robert had worked with on several occasions) wanted to meet us. He was a very pleasant guy and expressed a desire to give back to help people. Victor had been out of prison for five years and wanted to buy houses and flip them. He wanted to hire guys who couldn't find jobs because of their past and to use some of these homes to help people. Victor happened to have a Victorian-style duplex. One side was partially remodeled, and the other side needed to be fully remodeled.

God (through Victor) made me an offer I couldn't refuse. Victor said if he provided the finances and we helped him remodel the duplex, he would give us the place for six months, rent-free. He asked for no deposit and only $600 a month for both sides after six months. We knew this was only God, but I still didn't want to do this. Robert and a few brothers in his church worked during the day and the evening to remodel one side.

Carolina and I met with some deputy mayors, a city council member, and a few others to let them know we were opening this home. Everybody agreed if we got the home up and going, they would embrace this work. Raj was so happy when she heard about the home. Her mother was excited and gave us a check to help us. She looked into resources in the community and got us a bunch of furniture.

By the time Raj got out of the hospital, we had a place for her. Carolina and I didn't have a bed or anything in our room, and we knew it would be a time of sacrifice again. Raj got out of the hospital and said she met someone in the hospital who needed a place to stay and felt he would be an asset to the home. Jake turned out to be a jack-of-all-trades and was very instrumental in supervising the side jobs we would soon be doing. Surinder and

Raj introduced us to a few of their friends who would turn out to be a blessing to the home.

Unida International House of Restoration was now open. Things were moving quickly, so fast I couldn't keep up. God never ceases to amaze me. When God is in it, everything goes smoothly. All I could do at times was get on my knees and cry because of the awesomeness of Abba Father!

We met Pastor Del through Raj, and we attended his church. He and his wife, Ginger, played a big part in the program. We teamed up with Del and the Genesis Initiative. Ginger had a brother who owned a furniture company and donated bunk beds, dressers, and comforters [Thank you]. We also met Sam from Sam's Auto, who was a blessing in many ways to my wife, the home, and to me. We also met the Shahs, and our home received many side jobs through them. Thank you all for being a blessing to Unida!

Speaking of blessings, Raj, Surinder, and their beautiful family opened up their home to allow Carolina and me to have a church wedding. They paid for everything. Carolina wore one of their saris (an Indian dress) and we had a partial Indian wedding. Our son-in-law performed the wedding, and our daughter sang some songs. We were not just friends, we were family. Thank you, Raj, Surinder, Ashley Marie, and Mina.

We got involved in the community, and those in the home learned to give back and be servants. We started programs for the homeless, gangs, drug addicts, and alcoholics. About 95 percent of those in the homes were homeless. Throughout the decades of running homes, we rarely housed the homeless population. We realized the homeless population was probably the hardest type of person to accommodate.

Our homes had never charged rent up to this point. We found today's generation was totally different from times past. Everybody seemed to have an entitlement mentality. Everybody wanted everything for free. They didn't want to deal with authority, didn't want responsibility, and definitely didn't want to work. Some people were very deceitful, manipulative, and vindictive. Some guys tried to get us closed down. Most of those in the home complained about everything. At times, I felt as though we had a daycare for adults.

After about a year, a few guys were doing well. We met a young lady who rented us a duplex for a good price. We separated the two homes and had a Faith-Based home and a Clean and Sober home.

God brought a special couple into our lives, Bishop Derek Lamont Jefferson and First Lady Karen, along with the Jerusalem Temple family. We literally fell in love with our new family. God always brought good people to walk beside us.

Victor went to New York for a few days, was in an automobile accident, and passed away (RIP). His sister came to the home and made us an offer. She wanted us to live in the home rent-free. All we had to do was pay the property taxes. It was too good to be true, but that's the way God is.

Victor's sister said Victor loved our home so much and would like to be remembered for giving back. However, Victor's wife wanted to raise the rent. We were stuck in the middle and didn't want to be an inconvenience to anyone. We moved to the other duplex.

I got to know Bishop Jefferson. Carolina and I felt right at home. It felt good to be in a church where the Holy Spirit showed up and we had a Holy Ghost service. We just wanted to be a blessing to the church and the community.

Years before, my wife had accidentally poked herself with her ex-husband's needle and caught hepatitis-C and was about to start treatment. She was also diagnosed with fibromyalgia and became bedridden most of the time. After two and a half years, Carolina's mother received some bad news regarding her health. Carolina put the hep-C treatment on hold and my beautiful wife went to Colorado to be near her mother. After two weeks she came back, and I knew I would have to make a decision. I knew I had to be at my wife's side.

We went to Denver to stay with her mother and see what would happen and what we would have to do. Her mother was in the hospital for a few days and then was sent to rehab after chemotherapy. After the treatment, the lung cancer shrunk, but it spread to the bones and she was sent home for hospice. She was given a month, but she lived a little longer.

My wife had lived through some hard times in her life. She grew up being molested by the adults in her life, lost family members, was beaten by men, and did the best she could to raise her son alone. Right before we married, she was raped and left for dead, but the angels delivered her.

We were with her mother 24/7. The hospice company saw that my wife loved her mother so much and took care of her so well that they offered her a job. This was the hardest thing my wife had ever been through and the hardest thing she will possibly ever go through. This was the hardest time I ever had to go through as well. My wife stayed in the room with her mother day in and day out—taking care of her, praying, crying, and doing everything she could to make her mother comfortable. And through it all, she led her mother to the Lord.

This was the only time in my life when I didn't know what to do. I felt so helpless. What could I do? What could I say? All I could do was trust God and have faith that everything would be okay. I didn't know how to handle seeing my beautiful wife hurting so badly. We didn't know how long we would be there, whether we would go back to Indianapolis or stay here. We had to trust that God's providence and His plan superseded our thoughts, plans, and desires. I just knew that my wife needed me right next to her.

CHAPTER X

COME FULL CIRCLE (2015-2018)

God said, "It has been forty years. I have brought you through these forty years. Forty years of testing, transition, and probation are finished. I took you through this journey to see the heart of man and to prepare you to fulfill your calling."

Sally, my wife's mother, went home to be with the Lord. Carol was going to Las Vegas for a month to visit our mother and her son and asked us to come to Colorado Springs to help watch her house. She knew my wife and I were unsure of what to do. Carolina didn't want to go back to Indianapolis and leave our son, Teddy, our daughter-in-law, Kelly, and the grandkids (Ahlaya and Armani) again. Armani was born while we were in Indianapolis, and Ahlaya was growing. The grandmother in my beautiful wife wanted to be near her children, grandchildren, and her only sibling, Robert.

During the last few days of Sally's life, she asked my wife to make it a point to take care of Robert. This made it even harder to go back to Indianapolis. It was a very hard time for my wife, and I knew she would need all the support she could get. I knew she would need family.

As my sister was getting ready to go to Las Vegas, she and my nephew, Andrew, told us about a church nearby called Restoration Church. We went the very next Sunday. It was Pastor Paul Aragon's five-year anniversary, and he was speaking about the church's twenty-year vision. Part of the vision was a home they were considering closing.

My wife nudged me and said, "Babe, they have a home."

Once again, I said, "No more homes."

We met with Pastor Paul to see if we could do something and how we could fit in. They had a heart for helping people in need, but the experience level was low. Restoration House had been open for a few years. The contract with the couple who owned the two houses was just about to be renewed. My wife said, "Maybe we need to help Pastor Paul with this home." We talked about it, prayed about it, and made a proposal to Pastor Paul. We told him we would make a two-year commitment and then reevaluate the agreement. He was excited and said he would bring it to the Board of Directors.

We were introduced to the Board of Directors and shared our testimony and background, and everyone asked questions. They asked how much we wanted, but we said we didn't want pay. Never in all the twenty-four years of living in the homes had we ever received a paycheck because we have an awesome God, Jehovah-Jireh (our provider).

We met with the couple who owned the two small houses, but the houses were too small. We closed those homes and searched for a bigger house, praying for God's guidance and favor. Andrew was on the internet daily looking for something close to the church. One day, he called and said he had found a seven-bedroom, four-bathroom house located in a cul-de-sac. The house was a beautiful three-story that went up the hill with a huge backyard that looked like a forest.

I called to talk with Stan, the property manager. I didn't think a property management company would rent this place to a program, but we prayed about it and met with Stan. We were told that the first three homes in the cul-de-sac were built in the 1980s and were the first to be built in this development. The one we were looking at was called "The Judge."

This was the beginning of our time as directors of Restoration House. So we opened up the Faith-Based Program and the Clean and Sober Program. It wasn't very long before the home filled up.

We had many people in the Faith-Based portion of the home, and we wanted to be a blessing to Restoration Church and to the community. My wife and I had never worked with a Board of Directors, and it took a little while to adjust. This would all be new to us, to the church, and to the Board of Directors. I would like to thank the Board of Directors personally: Pastor Paul, Stephanie, Darryl, Alea, Christine, and Martin (RIP).

We found an abundance of friends and family at Restoration Church. When we announced the grand opening, we needed furniture. Within a week, the home was completely furnished, and then some. We received so much that we could bless a few families in need. [Thank you, Lord and Restoration Church,]. Among the family we have found in the church, we have friends like we've never had before. We would like to thank God for Brock, Amy, and their family.

We had been praying for the major cities on behalf of all the shootings and killings taking place. Chicago ranked number one. We contacted the mayor's office, gang unit, churches, and programs working with the gangs in Chicago to see if we could make a difference. Patrick from Nicky Cruz's Outreach, Art Blajos, Pastor Pepe and his drama, and a few pastors who had come out of the homes in the past were all ready to participate in the peace treaty.

My wife and I set a time to meet with some of these entities and went to Chicago a few times to work on a peace treaty. If we could make a difference in this city, that would be great. We found out it wasn't a peace treaty this city needed; it would take a mighty move of God! The shootings and killings were not gang retaliation as we were used to dealing with in the past. Something just didn't seem right. My wife kept saying she had an uneasy feeling about the whole situation.

It was too late to back out. I prayed for the Holy Spirit's guidance. I couldn't get any assistance from the government officials or the city officials. I had to rely on the churches and programs to pull this one off. The person meeting with us from the police department was in charge of the gang unit. He informed us that it wasn't a peace treaty we needed to focus on, and what he told us next just blew my mind.

One gang in Chicago was responsible for most of the shootings and killings. They weren't a regular gang. Their rules were gang members couldn't abuse drugs and alcohol and couldn't land on the wrong side of the law. They were to go to school and get educated to become lawyers, city council members, mayors, senators, congressmen, governors, or even the president of the United States to legalize drugs coming into the United States.

So each gang member was placed on a point system. Zero to 500 points were those who got arrested and went to prison. Those who received higher points were killed, and anyone around them was killed also. So I was unsure about how to deal with this.

All I could do was pray for God's will to be done. This definitely was not a peace treaty situation. This was turning out to be a political situation. Now it made sense; it was coming together. No wonder I couldn't get help from the city officials.

My wife and I were committed to going as far as it would take. A community event around this time had dozens of children, and someone began shooting. We set up another event the following month, but my wife and I couldn't make it because of prior commitments. A community activist was the speaker and ended up being shot and killed. Everything was canceled indefinitely, so that ended our participation.

Shortly after this, my wife would experience more pain and another death in her family. Through the years, she had tried to help Robert. He had been in our homes several times, and we did everything we could to help him. This time there was a difference; it seemed God had finally reached Robert. He went back to Denver but left his clothes at our home for about a month.

On a Friday, we took his clothes and belongings to him and talked to him for a few minutes. On Monday morning, my wife received a call that Robert was taken to the hospital. By the time she found out which hospital he was in, he had passed away. My wife found some letters written by Robert and addressed to God, which proved a change had taken place in his heart. It appeared that Robert had made his peace with God and felt secure in his salvation. Many of his friends came up for the altar call at his viewing night.

Immediately after Robert's death, we went back to Denver. Our niece, Christina, and husband, Arturo, agreed to come to Colorado Springs to be trained to run a women's home. Arturo came to Colorado Springs to begin his training. Our niece would join him a little later. Arturo gave his heart to the Lord and, a few days later, had to undergo emergency surgery. They held off on the surgery for twelve hours. My mother, my sister, Eva, and Christina were on their way to Colorado. They had no idea Arturo was about to pass away. It took everybody by surprise, but it was no surprise to God.

While we were dealing with the funeral plans for Robert in Denver, we were dealing with the funeral plans for Arturo in Pueblo. This was a very trying time, but we also experienced miracles. Shortly after this, my wife's favorite uncle, Butch, passed away, and shortly before his death, we led him to the Lord. Butch had always been like a brother to me.

We were nearing the end of the two-year commitment to Restoration House and the two-year contract on the property. Once again, I felt the Lord about to do something. One night I was lying in bed trying to get some sleep, tossing and turning, and the word "assignment" kept coming to mind. I got out of bed, went to the front room, and turned on the TV. A preacher was preaching on assignment. When the message ended, I changed the channel. Low and behold, another preacher was preaching on assignment. I said, "Okay, Father, this is not a coincidence. What are you trying to get across to me?"

I turned on some soft gospel music, lay down on my face before God, and sobbed. The Lord said, "Do you remember the night I spoke to you and told you what I was calling you to do?" I said yes and he asked me to repeat it. I told Him He said I was called to preach to a backslidden, stiff-necked, rebellious people, and to preach the message of the end times.

Then God asked me what year that was.

I said, "1976."

"Yes, it was 1976 and what is this year?"

"2016," I said.

He asked me how many years it had been from 1976 to 2016.

I said, "Forty years."

He said, "It has been forty years. I have brought you through these forty years. The forty years of testing, transition, and probation is finished. I took you through this journey to see the hearts of man and to prepare you to fulfill your calling. I am about to do a new thing in the life of you and your wife."

I told the Board of Directors that my wife and I were ready to retire from living in the homes and were ready to go on to what the Lord had in store. The Board of Directors voted to close the home if my wife and I wouldn't be there. We ended the contract on the property. We still had four guys in the home and my wife said, "We can't close the home and let these men go out on the streets."

So His love was birthed through all of this, and that was the last hoorah for my wife and me regarding the homes.

CONCLUSION

I intentionally left out people and situations in my life for the purpose of writing another book.

God has used each era in my life to prepare me for such a time as this. I know that we are in the last days and this is the purpose for which God has brought me full circle in my own life. I thought I missed it a few times, but God, in His infinite wisdom, knows what He is doing. "Full circle" means a series of developments that lead back to the original source, position, or situation or to a complete reversal of the original position.

My personal journey in life has been an amazing one. I thank God daily for His love, mercy, grace, guidance, provision, and protection. I've been asked if I were to be afforded an opportunity to do it all over again, what would I change? I don't believe I would change much. Along the way, I know I have hurt people and I have made mistakes. I have the heart of man beating inside of me. This is why God sent His only begotten Son into the world to die for us!

Jeremiah 17:9 – "The heart is deceitful above all things and beyond cure, who can understand it?"

Matthew 6:21 – "For where your treasure is, there your heart will be also."

Proverbs 4:23 – "Above all else, guard your heart, for everything you do flows from it."

Proverbs 23:26 – "My son, give me your heart and let your eyes delight in my ways."

Psalm 51:10 – "Create in me a pure heart, O, God, and renew a steadfast spirit within me."

Psalm 26:2 – "Test me Lord and try me, examine my heart and my mind."

If I have hurt anyone in any way, please forgive me!

As I look back over the years, I see the awesomeness of God. I am in awe. Only God can orchestrate the events in someone's life, to mold and shape a life to fit into His perfect will and allow us to obtain the prize of the high calling. Who are we that God should even care about us, much less be patient with us, forgive us, and strive with us? If I were God, I would've given up on me a long time ago! Thank you, Lord, for searching, molding, and shaping my heart through the years.

Proverbs 21:1-2 – "The King's heart is a stream of water in the hand of the Lord; He turns it wherever He will. Every way of man is right in his own eyes, but the Lord weighs the heart."

God hardened Pharaoh's heart. He will use the past, present, and future and people, places, and things. God will do this because He can! He is the Potter and we are the clay! Many scriptures in the Bible speak about the divine providence of God. The timely preparation for future eventualities, the foresight, the forethought of God never ceases to amaze me!

Sometimes in this thing we call life, we can become like a puzzle with all the pieces scattered all over. But like a puzzle, God can pick up the pieces, kiss them softly, and put them back together! I pray that this book will be inspiring to someone. That maybe someone can relate to what I've been through in life.

God is good!

Please, if you don't know the Lord as your personal Savior, or if you are backslidden and away from God, ask Him into your heart! He can and will make a difference in your life.

www.ingramcontent.com/pod-product-compliance
Lightning Source LLC
Chambersburg PA
CBHW022009120526
44592CB00034B/759